CROSSING THE WATERS

Rosemarie Sumira

ATHENA PRESS
LONDON

CROSSING THE WATERS
Copyright © Rosemarie Sumira 2007

All Rights Reserved

ISBN (10-digit): 1 84401 828 8
ISBN (13-digit): 978 1 84401 828 4

First Published 2007 by
ATHENA PRESS
Queen's House, 2 Holly Road
Twickenham TW1 4EG
United Kingdom

Printed for Athena Press

CROSSING THE WATERS

My heartfelt thanks go to my friends at the Thursday Writing Group: Agnes, Betty, Elizabeth and Pat, who encouraged me to persist in writing my memoirs

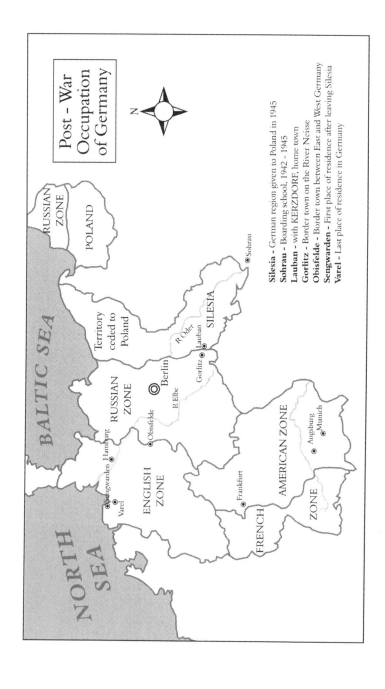

Post – War
Occupation
of Germany

N

BALTIC SEA

NORTH
SEA

RUSSIAN
ZONE

POLAND

Territory
ceded to
Poland

RUSSIAN
ZONE

Hamburg

Sengwarden

Varel

Obisfelde

ENGLISH
ZONE

Berlin

R Elbe

Gorlitz

R Oder

Lauban

SILESIA

Sohrau

Frankfurt

FRENCH

AMERICAN ZONE

ZONE

Augsburg

Munich

Silesia - German region given to Poland in 1945
Sohrau - Boarding school, 1942 - 1945
Lauban - with KERZDORF, home town
Gorlitz - Border town on the River Neisse
Obisfelde - Border town between East and West Germany
Sengwarden - First place of residence after leaving Silesia
Varel - Last place of residence in Germany

Author's Note

I was born in August 1927 in Kerzdorf, Lauban, in Silesia, which was then still a German province.

My parents, master baker Karl König and his wife Else named me Anna Ida Rosemarie, Anna and Ida being my grandmothers' Christian names and Rosemarie my main call name. However, some people in England know me as Anna.

After an idyllic childhood and comparatively non-traumatic war years, life turned into a nightmare for me and my family, when peace should have prevailed.

I came to work in England as a domestic help in 1949, and have lived here ever since. Gaining professional qualifications and an Open University degree enabled me later to become a nurse tutor and a lecturer in higher education settings, from where I retired in 1987.

I was widowed after forty-two years of marriage. My daughter is a globe restorer in London and my son a general practitioner in Northamptonshire.

I dedicate this book to them.

Part One

Home Ground

A Journey into the Past

The Berolina tour of East Germany seemed to provide a good opportunity to introduce my daughter to parts of Germany that were not on the usual tourist trails. I hoped to take her a little further eastward as well.

Hans, our tour guide in Dresden, was lost for words when I told him that we would not go on the river trip planned for the next day, but intended to travel to Poland to see what was left of the place I grew up in, and what had been my family home. He had obviously not encountered obstreperous tourists like us before, who interfered with the carefully mapped out itinerary of this East Germany tour, and with the rules and regulations which he felt ought to be obeyed without question – like not straying from the beaten track, and having passports available to look at and to stamp whenever we went to a different location.

I assured him that we had obtained the required exit and entrance permits in London – from the DDR and Polish consulates – and could not see any reasons why we should encounter any difficulties in transit and when crossing the borders in both directions.

It was only about forty miles to the East German/Polish border and Lauban, my former hometown, was not more than fifteen miles beyond this. We had actually bought our tickets already and no one at the Dresden Hauptbahnhof had queried our intentions. Sixteen marks (about five pounds at the time) seemed to be a ridiculously small sum to pay for a ticket to a place that had been inaccessible so far and, from England, seemed thousands of miles away. From Dresden, the Warsaw Express would take less than two hours to get us there.

Hans was still not convinced that we were doing the right thing, but, realising that we were determined to have our way and that he could not physically stop us from going, he had to be reassured that we would not hold him responsible for anything that might go wrong. We were to report to him the moment we returned. He would not be able to rest otherwise.

The exterior of the Hauptbahnhof had been restored to a degree after the ravages of the bombing raids at the end of the war, but there the glamour ended. Money for repair and upkeep of buildings was scarce in the Eastern Bloc. There was a lot of labour-intensive sweeping going on, but this did not have a marked impact on the general decay and shabbiness of the ticket hall, the waiting areas, the platforms and what experts call 'the rolling stock'.

We had not expected anything as stylish as the Orient Express, but the Warsaw Express, exotic as it sounded, was a definite disappointment. It consisted of a motley collection of pre-war carriages, which had obviously seen better days. One showed remnants of the maroon shade of a *Mitropa* wagon, once considered to be the height of luxury in railway catering.

This was definitely the train we had to board. The chipped metal boards on the side of the wagons indicated its destination: Warsaw via Zgorzelec (Görlitz), Jelenia Gora, Wroclaw. Lauban, now named Luban Slask, on to which my home village Kerzdorf bordered, would be a minor station between the first two major towns.

Without the encumbrance of luggage we could at least look for, and find, a reasonably clean and comfortable corner inside, but even there the plastic upholstery was grimy, and wherever one went one could not get away from the smell of cheap tobacco and the stench of stale urine which emanated from the end of the carriage. Apart from two cigar-smoking men with gold teeth and very smart leather briefcases, we were the only occupants of the coach.

The whistle sounded, and we moved off exactly on time – passing through part of the ruined old town and over the Elbe Bridge, from where we could see some of the still splendid Baroque royal palaces beyond the wide terrace above the river, which a poet once called the 'Balcony of Europe'. People were busy in the fields as we passed through agricultural landscapes. Some children even waved.

The ticket collector came, a jovial Pole who beamed and bowed to us, inquiring what made us want to go to Lauban. A somewhat sterner customs official followed. We felt just a little apprehensive as he scrutinised our papers minutely, taking much time over this. There were obviously not many passengers who went on day trips to Poland with British passports and visas issued in London. Still, our '*documenta*' must have been to his satisfaction, because he stamped them, having made some notes in triplicate. We got one of the copies, and had our passports returned as the serious young man clicked his heels and wished us '*djen dobre*'. I thought only Germans clicked their heels.

Then another uniformed man entered the compartment with a locked briefcase. He demanded to see the forms we had been given, as well as our passports, and indicated that he was authorised to change the obligatory sum of 'hard' currency into zloties. Foreigners entering Poland had to change a set amount of their pounds, marks or dollars for every day they intended to stay in the country. Any foreign money still in our possession after the exchange had to be counted and listed on entry and shown on exit from Poland to make sure we had not entered in money marketeering in the East. People in the know could get a much more favourable exchange rate within the country than what was officially given on the train. This would not have been of any benefit to us since we found it difficult to spend our one-day non-returnable zloty allocation. Boiled potatoes, a kind of rissole and cucumber salad for lunch came cheap. There was only one type of postcard of Lauban available and we were only allowed to buy two of these. I was able to get some stamps when I saw that the post office was still in its old location. There was nothing else to buy which was of interest to us in local shops. However, illegally imported pounds, marks or dollars could have bought almost anything, including huge bottles of spirits or designer briefcases on the black market.

These official procedures left us longing for a soothing cup of tea, but we had to settle for a glass of coffee, the only non-alcoholic drink available from the Mitropa car. Coffee? Was this murky liquid served in dumpy glass tumblers really coffee? It was not the sort of beverage we were used to, neither was it anything like Turkish coffee, except for its grainy texture. No milk was available, but sugar was offered, which made the liquid even more disgusting. I noticed that the gold-toothed men fortified their coffee with a generous measure of vodka, but we preferred to keep our heads clear for later. We had reached the border by then, where the officials alighted, locking the carriage doors behind them.

Nothing happened for a while as we stood in no-man's-land. Then the shunting started. Another steam engine was attached, and eventually puffed its way slowly over the high level bridge, which spanned the river. The Neisse looked quite insignificant among the greenery far below. Few could have guessed that it was of great historic importance – achieving notoriety when it became the line where the formerly German Silesia was severed from the rest of Germany to become a Polish province.

We reached our destination less than forty minutes later. Some familiar landmarks appeared, but once we left the train it came as a shock to me to realise how thorough the Poles had been in obliterating traces of its German past. Street names, directions and shop signs were in Polish, and nobody spoke German. It was just as well that I remembered the way to the places I wanted to show my daughter – no questions needed to be asked or answered as we embarked on a rather nostalgic, somewhat painful, journey through the past.

Eventually, we managed to bribe an off-duty taxi driver to take us to the top of the Steinberg, a hill overlooking the town. He could not understand what we wanted at first, but gestures, a picture on our newly acquired postcard and waving a bundle of zloties about helped the communication process. In next to no time, we reached the top of the promontory from where we had a prime view of what I once called home: Kerzdorf and its environment.

From a distance, it looked as if nothing had changed in the thirty-eight years since I saw the village last. Although the trees had grown to maturity and the shrubs on the hillside had thickened, it was still possible to catch a glimpse of my home ground from the vantage point on the Steinberg where we sat – the site of many happy outings and picnics during my childhood.

The River Queis glistened in the afternoon sun as it meandered through the foothills of the Sudeten Mountains, which, on a clear day like that, were sharply outlined against the pale blue sky. Red and grey roofs peeped through luscious greenery and the major landmarks could still be defined: the mansion of Count Strachwitz on the left beyond the railway lines, the river and the red-roofed brick fortification, the *Unterwerk*, which had once housed the machinery and switchgear ensembles for the electrified rail lines along the Sudeten Mountains and towards the Czech border. The branch line to Marklissa wound its way past our back garden. I can still hear the tinkling bell of the small train as it approached and left the stations on the way: Kerzdorf, Holzkirch, Steinkirch and so on. I always thought that it was rather strange that the church in Holzkirch ('wood church') was built of stone while the church in Steinkirch ('stone church') had a wooden tower. We could just about see them beyond the last houses of the village.

The sturdy schoolhouse seemed to be still there, next to a low-slung, newer building, standing on the land of the former village gardener, who supplied not only vegetables, fruit and berries in season from a ramshackle shed but also pot plants and flowers for all occasions. Customers could roam the terrain and dig bedding plants out for themselves if they wanted to beautify their gardens, or the graves in the nearby cemetery.

The cemetery walls looked as solid as ever, surmounted by huge lime trees. From there a path led to the old brickworks and on to the sloping meadow where once a year, as part of a colourful village feast, a competition took place to find the best shot in the village. He would then reign as 'king' for the next year, and preside over the meetings and social activities of the shooting guild, to which all village males aspired to belong. My father had been the proud owner of this title on more than one occasion.

Woodland seemed to have swallowed up the old quarry next to the shooting galleries, but the newer quarry had expanded towards the village and had almost reached the site of the open-air swimming pool that the villagers had built themselves in the 1930s. It was then, and during the war years, an almost indispensable meeting place for old and young. Many a romance blossomed there during the long summers. There was no sign of the large expanse of water – at least we could not see it behind the huge mulberry trees and bushes. The mulberries were once the suppliers of fodder for the silkworm farm, which was started in the village school to aid the war effort via the production of parachute silk.

There had always been more than enough volunteers to gather mulberry leaves during school hours, usually linked with a furtive dip in the pool. In winter, when the water froze over, we skated there if we were not practising downhill skiing or daring slalom runs on the hillside on our primitive skis.

The sound of throbbing machinery drifted up from the quarry. I wondered if they still had lunchtime detonations, preceded by the piercing sounds of sirens that warned the workers in the opencast area to shelter from the disintegrating rocks. On hot, dry days when the wind blew from the west, paths and meadows in the area, and even the manager's house, were covered with fine grey stone dust. It still seemed to be so.

I would have liked to believe that this almost idyllic vista still represented home, but I knew that this was an illusion.

Later, we walked along the once familiar village streets and alleys. They were potholed, weed-infested and labelled with strange Polish names. Houses left in ruins after the war had been flattened, with trees and bushes filling the gaps. Only some of the remaining houses seemed to be occupied and showed signs of life. Others, including our family home, were shuttered and neglected. Our sturdy, ornate shop door had withstood the test of time and lack of care. There were even some vestiges of the green paint left behind the rusting metal bars that kept us out. Incongruously, the house number, a brilliant white '12', shone as brightly as ever.

We did not meet anyone on our way. The silence was over-whelming. There were no voices or animal sounds from what had once been prosperous farms. There was certainly no traffic noise, not even the sound of a bicycle bell to be heard. What I missed most were the once familiar sounds of the rattling sewing machines of the home workers, who on a hot sunny day like this would have flung their windows open while they hemmed their handkerchiefs for the textile firms in Lauban.

We had intended to have some refreshments on the way, but

there were no welcoming inns as there had been. We could not even find an open shop – in fact, the place was like a ghost village. Denuding it of its native German population after the war seemed to have sapped its life and soul.

It was so different when I was young.

The family bakery, 1902

The shop door, 1984 – 'No Entry'

At Home in Kerzdorf

Until 1945 Kerzdorf was an unpretentious but quite prosperous village of about 1,700 inhabitants. It bordered directly on Lauban, the county town, but had its own *Bürgermeister*, fire station, school, post office and cemetery, complete with gravedigger and undertaker. The one and only policeman was more than able to cope with the occasional aberrations of the otherwise law-abiding citizens. He knew everybody and was very approachable, but would not tolerate any nonsense. Anyone found to be drunk and disorderly or engaged in any kind of vandalism was taken to the cell next to his office, where the culprit was given time to reflect on his behaviour before being released with a warning. If there were any more severe crimes than that, I was not aware of them.

Kerzdorf was well supplied with shops, catering for the needs of daily living. Three butchers vied with each other to produce the tastiest sausages. The five bakers, including my father, had their local clientele but also their own specialities. Baker Wunsch had the most modern baking oven and could produce finer patisseries than our old oven, installed nearly eighty years earlier, could do. Ours had to be fed with wood and coal through an ornate, cast iron metal door till the fuel glowed fiercely. Metal plates were then slid over the glowing embers and the bread or rolls to be baked were placed on the hot metal with long wooden paddles. A lot of skill and experience was required to judge the correct temperature. Later, when Father acquired a more modern baking oven, he was able to expand his range of products to rival anyone's.

Several *Kolonialwarenladen* (grocers) sold anything from flypapers to sauerkraut. The *Molkerei* specialised in dairy products. People brought their own milk cans there to be filled or to a cart, which made a daily round through the village. The tobacconist had a phone for general use. He could also summon a taxi from Lauban for special occasions.

The three inns also had their own characteristics: Hieke's, in the middle of the village, was not a place to which ladies would go alone, but Pfohl's 'Golden 44' had an attractive garden near the River Queis, popular for ladies' gatherings and birthday parties. Postler's not only had several public rooms for drinking and card playing, but also a ballroom where dances were held from time to time and which could be hired for meetings, weddings, large dinner parties and other occasions like concerts, plays and the annual school show.

Fräulein Preis sold threads, buttons, buckles and ribbons, and the two cobblers also sold shoes and plimsolls, but for clothing, household items and luxury goods, we had to go to Lauban, which, with its three cinemas, cafes and dance halls, provided entertainment opportunities for various tastes.

There were two large farming estates in Kerzdorf as well as about half a dozen smaller family-run farms and smallholdings and a versatile market gardener. The large *Reichsbahnausbesserungswerk*, a state-owned rail repair and maintenance workshop, was within easy walking distance of the village and employed hundreds of men in different capacities. Flax was grown in the area. Several spinning and weaving factories produced fine linen and specialised in handkerchief making, exporting these goods all over the world, thus giving rise to the saying that *Lauban putzt der ganzen Welt die Nase* (Lauban wipes the whole world's nose.) Many women worked in this industry, some of them as out-workers. Many housewives earned some extra money that way. Villagers who did not work locally in shops, farms, the basalt quarry or the brickworks could easily find employment in Lauban.

We had a number of excellent craftsmen in the village: a smith, a plumber and a joiner. The *Ofensetzer* could build and maintain the tiled stoves, the main form of heating in the houses. Stefan, the grocer, repaired bicycles as a sideline. I can't remember anyone being unemployed. Even 'Stummy', a hydrocephalic, and so-called village idiot, found things to do. He had a little handcart that he used to take bales of handkerchiefs to homeworkers for finishing. He also wheeled some people's laundry baskets to Fischers' or Arnolds' house. They had a huge mangle that would flatten sheets and towels and other uncomplicated items by sheer brute force. The mangle consisted of a sturdy wooden box, about two by four metres, filled with stones. This could be moved to and fro over what looked like huge rolling pins, around which the items to be flattened had been wound. We sometimes helped to turn the wheel, which moved the stone box to and fro on ratchets. Eventually Herr Emmerich, the electrician, installed a heated mangle on his premises, which was much superior but more expensive to use.

A few villagers had their own houses or cottages, but most of them lived in flats. The flats the rail authority built for their employees were quite modern, with water closets and taps on the landings. We also had a piped water supply, but were quite content with our outside toilets – one for the family with a small seat for children, and one for staff members and visitors. Farmer Enders came from time to time to pump out the brick-built waste container and used the contents to fertilise his fields. Primitive as some facilities might have been, we coped well with whatever was available to us. I can't remember anyone feeling deprived or disadvantaged. Kerzdorf was a most congenial place to live in while we were able to do so.

Growing up in Kerzdorf was a good experience. We lived in a solid, big house that was always kept warm and cosy by the baking oven at its core. The shop was next to the bakery and the sitting room next to the shop, so that Mother could keep an eye on us while serving the customers. In summer, if the doorbell was quiet for a while, she sat at her little sewing table near the open window exchanging greetings with passers-by. In winter, when the double windows had been fixed to the outside of the house to keep the freezing air out, the low bench near the tiled stove was her favourite resting place before more customers demanded attention.

Behind the shop and across the flagged hall lay the kitchen, with its built-in stove, which served also as a water heater. Steaming hot water could be directed into the washing-up bowls at the turn of the brass tap. A pot of grain coffee was kept constantly warm in the heated chamber in the side of the stove. A large, square, pine table and wooden benches served as working and eating areas during the week. Only on Sundays, when there was less flour dust about, was the draw-leaf table in the sitting room extended and covered with a white linen cloth. It was then large enough to accommodate the family, the bakers and Grandmother, who lived upstairs, and possibly also one or two guests for the midday and evening meal. Mother was considered to be an excellent cook, able to cater for large numbers with a minimum of fuss. She was famous for her roasts, spiced red cabbage and potato dumplings.

Next to the kitchen was a small, vaulted room with a battered, but very comfortable leather settee. Father rested there after lunch when the day's baking, that started in the middle of the night, had been done. We loved this place as children, a sentiment shared by two cousins, and later by school friends who spent a lot of time with us. When the doorway curtain was drawn, we felt in a little world of our own in there, playing games, telling stories, dressing up or even staging small entertainments. The drapes would then be dramatically opened to whatever audience happened to be in the kitchen, while we sang, recited poems or performed sketches. Much later, when Father acquired a modern baking oven, the little vault was converted into a splendid bathroom – the envy of the neighbourhood. The old tin bath, formerly used for bathing in the kitchen, became redundant.

Grandmother had her own flat upstairs after Grandfather died. The sweeping staircase also led to four bedrooms on the first floor, and to a couple of storerooms. These always smelled exquisitely of dried apples and herbs. Sealed glass jars full of cherries, plums, berries and other garden produce were lined up on wooden shelves there, while other provisions like crates of potatoes, gherkins and bins full of sauerkraut were kept in the small cellar. This flooded at times when the snow melted in the mountains or heavy storms caused the river to overflow. Occasionally a bottle of fermenting beer burst and caused another kind of flood, with glass splinters making barefoot excursions into the cellar a dangerous undertaking.

More stairs led up to the attic, with its rooms for the bakers, and odd little nooks and crannies crammed with old chests and fascinating oddments, like Grandmother's old hats and fur muffs, and the broken old music box and its spiked metal disks. A huge pear tree had grown on the south wall of the house and reached up to the eaves so that we could pick pears from one of the attic windows in autumn.

We had a large garden and fields behind the house, adjoining the railway line. A local farmer worked the land for us, using a kind of crop rotation: potatoes, rye or oats, and turnips and cabbages occupied different parts of the acres in turn. The fields were later purchased by the government, since the site, having access to rail transport, was eminently suitable for an army depot for clothing and appliances needed at the Eastern Front during the war. However, we were still left with a large garden with apple and plum trees of all descriptions, beds for herbs and vegetables, and what amounted to a plantation of redcurrants, far too many for just home and shop use. Surplus berries ordered by and sold to regular customers provided some pocket money for Mother in the summer. Unlike us children, Grandmother and some elderly neighbours seemed to like spending summer afternoons picking berries, sitting on little stools and gossiping the time away in anticipation of their coffee and cake rewards when the required number of punnets had been filled.

It was safe to play in the garden, where we had a huge sand-box, and swings suspended from the largest branch of an apple tree. We could hide, or tell ghost stories in a narrow, dark, damp passage between two outbuildings where we could also scrape white flakes, exuded from the old brickwork, to use as a plausible icing substitute for our sand pies or make-believe marble babas. In the summer, Father filled a big tin bath with water for us to dip and splash in before we were old enough to join the older children in the local swimming pool.

The large covered yard, with vehicle and coal sheds on one side, and pigsties, a wash house and the little and large outside toilets on the other, provided a great play area on rainy days. We never had an inside toilet – we did not even know that such modern contraptions existed until we began to experience the wider world.

Part Two

Glimpses of Childhood

Parents and Ancestors

Mother and Father grew up only a few miles from each other, yet it was twenty-two years before they met and discovered common ground.

Mother came from farming stock, but her father, my grandfather, had to abandon his farm after a fire and later worked as a groom and coachman on a large estate near Lauban. He found a little flat in this town for his family. Grandmother worked as a cleaner in the nearby convent to help make ends meet in bringing up a family of four sons and a daughter. Mother could not remember much of living on the farm, other than that it was definitely more roomy and gracious than their town flat. This faced a huge backyard where the monumental mason who owned the house had his workshop and displayed his tombstones. We found this fascinating when visiting and also marvelled at the mini rail-track, which ran through the large entrance hall of the building. Sturdy, flat-topped wagons were used to transport stone and marble blocks to the mason's workshop and finished tombstones and plaques to the street door for delivery to their destinations.

Mother's older brother, Oscar, at the age of about five or six was run over by a truck, carrying a winged angel, injuring both his legs severely. He would have loved to become a professional soldier like his three brothers, but was declared unfit for service because of his permanent limp. He became a barber instead.

When the First World War broke out and Oscar's assistant was called up, Mother began to help in his shop after school. She showed considerable talent for the job and began to do ladies' hair when waving and shingling became fashionable. She had a little portable spirit stove on which the curling tongs could be heated. It was still used at times later to do friends and relatives a favour for weddings and other festivities that merited special hairdos.

A visitor from Berlin suggested that she could develop her

skills further and do well for herself by joining a theatrical company she was connected with as a coiffeur. It was a tempting offer, and eventually she took the plunge and started to work in territory totally alien to a young, provincial girl. Still, she stood her ground, earned her own living and supported her family at home while working in Berlin, Hamburg and later in Spindelmühle, a ski resort in the Sudeten Mountains.

She found a job in a Jewish family firm, who actually had a Ladies' Hair Salon and supplied a peripatetic hairdresser, my mother, to local hotels, where the German and Czech elite spent their winter sports holidays. It was in this resort that she met my Father.

He was the son of a well-established master baker in Kerzdorf. He came from a family of six children: three boys and three girls. The youngest son died of diphtheria as a small child. Another, Fritz, was shot when working as a mining engineer in southern Germany, allegedly because of jealousy. That left Father the only surviving son to carry on the family trade.

Father had wanted to be a teacher, but since his two brothers died young and there was no one else to take over the well-established family business, he agreed, somewhat reluctantly, to learn the trade when he returned home from the traumas of the First World War. If he ever resented or regretted this choice, he did not show it – in fact, people saw him to be a contented, prosperous businessman, who truly knew his job and won acclaim and prizes for his products.

I can still see him, at the end of a busy morning, leaning against the white enamel panels of his state-of-the-art baking oven, newly installed when the old brick oven ceased to be able to meet the demands of Father's ever increasing range of bakery products. From this stance he tended to survey the arena of his activities, left hand resting on his hip, right hand holding the first cigarette of the morning, to be savoured before getting on with the rest of the day.

Having worked since the middle of the night, he looked tired but also content, taking in the scent of the freshly baked bread and the sight of the crusty rye loaves and the more refined white baguettes, waiting on trays, ready to be taken to the shop or to the carrying baskets for delivery elsewhere. His face and hair would be dusted with flour, as were his grey cotton trousers and singlet, and the white apron he wore.

On bright days, sunbeams would light up the flour dust suspended in the air, and paint pretty patterns onto the terrazzo floor where bowls and wooden dough troughs were piled high, waiting to be scrubbed.

Leaving his leather sandals behind, Father then went to the washroom, to rid himself of the traces of his trade, looking forward to lunch and grain coffee, or occasionally a glass of beer. A couple of hours of rest would follow and then the social part of the day began, while Mother was left in charge of the shop and domestic affairs in general.

He used to take us into the garden when we were children, to show us how to sow, plant and tend the vegetables he liked: beans, peas, kohlrabi, lettuce and kale, and little red radishes which grew very fast and tasted delicious when sliced and laid on buttered rye bread.

He taught us to swim before we went to school. He was the president of the local swimming club. There were galas and competitions in summer, and dances and hotpot suppers in winter when even the hardiest members of the club dared not brave the icy waters of the river or, later, the outdoor pool.

An active member of the Bakers' Guild he sang in the choir and acted in the amateur dramatic group. The latter met at our house at times to rehearse some scenes for their annual carnival offering. My brother and I once eavesdropped when we should have been in bed. We could not believe our eyes when we saw Father in a silk dress and a wig, causing hilarity amongst the assembled actors. He loved the limelight and entertaining people – which Mother and we found somewhat embarrassing, but others seemed to enjoy.

It was not unusual for him to be asked to be Master of Ceremonies at local weddings and other festive occasions. He was known for his repertoire of humorous speeches, anecdotes, piano ditties and opera songs, and ways to gain audience participation, especially charming the ladies in the process and causing Mother pangs of jealousy.

When no special occasions beckoned, he sought the company of the regulars at Postler's pub to play cards (skat, usually) and drink Pilsener with corn chasers, losing track of time and sobriety more than once. Mother hated these bouts of abandon, knowing well how difficult it would be to wake him during the night to start baking. Still, the rolls might have been a little late in the shop – people started buying fresh rolls from 7 a.m. onwards – but he never abandoned his customers totally. 'Work hard and play hard' seemed to be the philosophy he lived by. He expressed this at times by reciting a ballad he learned from a topical entertainer of the 1930s. Each verse, which could be tailored to the occasion, ended with the refrain: 'We might as well live it up now – in fifty years it's all over anyway.

August, his father, my grandfather, remained in control of the business well into the 1920s. He was a much-respected villager with a real presence. During the war he duped military guards on the railway bridge by telling them that they had no right to stop him, because he was König August, König (King) being our family name. The soldiers should have known that King August had been dead for many years, but, in ignorance, they stood to attention and saluted while Grandfather took the forbidden shortcut to the Eagle, one of the inns he liked to frequent.

Anna, my grandmother on Father's side, was a stately, beauti-fully-dressed woman, who for some reason felt a little superior to the rest of the village folk. She did not really like running the shop, serving customers, weighing flour and yeast, etc. Her daughters were roped in to do shop duties at the earliest opportu-nity. They liked it, and resented the fact that my mother wanted to get involved in the business after her marriage to Father. How could a hairdresser possibly take on the work they had done so successfully over the years? Being charming and quite diplomatic, Mother won them over eventually. My arrival, and that of my brother a year later, helped to mollify the König women further.

Soon after that, Hanne, father's oldest sister, married Rudolf, who had had the bright idea of becoming a car dealer to the rich landowners in the area. There were no such things as car showrooms at the time. Once he had sold cars to Count Strachwitz and his coterie, he set up his own workshop to service and repair cars. Tante Hanne became very superior after that, and only came by chauffeur-driven car to visit us.

Her sister, Lene, married an engineer from the local rail repair workshop, one of the big employers in the area. Her family lived next door and their children teamed up with us to make an almost inseparable foursome till the end of our school days.

Grete, my youngest aunt, met and married Ossie, the great love of her life. He had a horrendous motorbike accident involving one of Hanne's drivers and died of gas gangrene on the day of my christening, when he should have been one of my godfathers. Grete, although a beauty, never married again, and became a bookkeeper in one of the handkerchief factories in Lauban. The job paid quite a lot of money, allowing her to take fancy skiing holidays and go on cruises, bringing back such exotic things as grapefruit and English marmalade. She held Hanne responsible for Ossie's death. The sisters eventually made it up when Hanne's only son was killed in the war, and post-war chaos caused established support systems to crumble.

The König and Buhl families had lived within a radius of no more than three miles from each other till the war ended. War and the post-war separation of Silesia from the rest of Germany caused us to be scattered all over the country. Since normal lines of communication did not exist at the time, it took months or even years to find out who had survived and if so, where they lived.

We never found out what happened to Grandma Buhl. Someone said that she had sought shelter in the convent where she had worked in her younger days, when the Russians took Lauban. The convent was totally destroyed, with no survivors to give information.

Mother's soldier brothers had gone rapidly up the ranks during the war. Erich, the eldest, was reported missing in Russia at the same time that his wife and three young children vanished in Dresden during the 'fire storm' in February 1945. Fritz was captured by the Russians and made to work in uranium mines for some years. He did not return to his family, living in Stuttgart till 1949, and later died of lung cancer. Gerhard lived the longest, working as a customs officer at one of the transit points of the Iron Curtain. Oscar died of old age at his daughter's home in Mönchengladbach.

Father's sisters settled in the Rhineland after Grandmother's death, and built themselves a small bungalow in their fifties, digging the foundations themselves to save cost. They lived to a ripe old age. My parents were not so lucky. After traumatic years in Polish-occupied Kerzdorf and expulsion in 1947, they established a new existence in Dresden, even running a rented bakery again. However, post-war trauma left them in poor health. Both died while still in their sixties.

My brothers and cousins, living in various parts of Germany and abroad, meet up from time to time. Inevitably thoughts turn to the past and the colourful characters who were our ancestors and who shaped and enriched our outlook on life.

Grandfather August Köning and
Cousin Christa

Grandmother Ida Köning

Father and his sisters: Grete, Hanne and Lene, 1918

Mother's family, the Buhls, 1914

Parents' wedding, 1925

Births and Birthdays

Mother always said that she was glad that I was born early in the morning, because she could not have survived another stifling hot August day in her bulky condition.

The midwife had been summoned during the night and Dr Fraenkel, our family doctor, soon followed as it became apparent that the labour was not progressing smoothly enough. The thought of sending Mother to hospital did not seem to have occurred to anyone. Instead, Dr Fraenkel got his forceps out and, with the help of a whiff of ether for his patient and a lot of skill on his part, pulled me into the world on the chaise longue in my parents' bedroom, while Father carried on with his routine tasks in the bakery. He found just enough time now and then to brew some 'proper' coffee, instead of the usual malted grain, to refresh the labour team upstairs.

My arrival was apparently a most desirable event, which not only pleased my parents but also did a lot to pacify Father's sisters, who had at first considered my mother to be a quite unsuitable intruder into their solidly established family. After all – whoever had then, in the early 1920s, had heard of a slip of a girl leaving home at sixteen to earn her own living in 'wicked' places like Berlin and Hamburg?

Grandfather apparently liked the girl that his only surviving son brought home, but it took time for Mother to convince the rest of the family that she could run a home and a business as well as any of them. Not only was she efficient but she was also very popular with her customers, the villagers as a whole, with Father's apprentices and with Elfriede, the country girl who came to help her when, a year after me, my brother Werner was born.

He arrived two months early and, nowadays, would have been treated in an incubator. No such fuss in the late 1920s. He was swaddled in flannel blankets and kept warm near the tiled stove, with a steaming kettle nearby to help his breathing. For a lightweight baby, he was a greedy feeder once he had learned where the milk came from. He soon gained weight.

For many years after, the remnants of a bottle of Franzbrantwein stood in our medicine cabinet. This had been used to massage his tiny limbs and back to strengthen them. It must have been effective, since he soon caught up in development and grew into a sturdy toddler and close companion for me.

Eight years later, in 1936, Karlheinz was born. Werner and I felt quite grown-up compared with the little bundle who, out of the blue, came into our life. Of course, he was too young to be included in some of our spare time activities like swimming and exploring our environment, in fact we seem to have seen and treated him like our latest pet. We called him Männel, little man, a name that stuck to him, to his chagrin, well into his school years.

The sun always shone on childhood birthdays, at least that is what I remember. Sun, August warmth, an expanse of garden and some established traditions were the basic ingredients of these memorable feasts, which gave the opportunity for an annual get-together of friends and family.

I usually had about a dozen young guests, cousins, school friends and neighbours' children, who trundled in by three o'clock with gift-wrapped parcels and in their Sunday best. This definitely was not the ideal way to dress for the occasion, which not only included decorous sitting around the table for the German equivalent of English afternoon tea, but also quite boisterous games to follow.

The linen-covered table was set under the largest apple tree to keep the tantalising concoctions on it in the shade: jugs with lemonade and home-made raspberry cordial, marble babas with thick chocolate icing, crisp cream horns and *Pflaumenkuchen* with whipped cream. There was also a wobbly mound of gaudily coloured *Götterspeise*, 'food for the gods', more prosaically known as fruit jelly, to be eaten with cold vanilla sauce.

We did not have a specific type of birthday cake, and the song 'Happy Birthday' was not known to us, but there were little speeches and poems and toasts like '*Hoch soll sie leben*' (Long may she live), followed by cheers.

One would have thought that gorging on all the sweet offerings from the table would result in relaxed satiation for the rest of the afternoon, but not so. We were encouraged to play a paper game, like 'Uncle sits in the bathtub', to let the food settle, but energy levels seemed to rise rapidly thereafter, making us itch to get on with more active games. Obstacle races and sack hopping were popular. Father lent us his wind-up gramophone, provided that a responsible person was operating it. We danced and moved about. When the music stopped we had to freeze in the position we found ourselves in. It was usually Grandfather who judged the most graceful or most unusual 'statue'. Everyone craved a prize. There were pencil sharpeners, hair ribbons or surprise bags with sweets and novelty gifts, such as spinning tops or bracelets.

While our caretaker's attention was being taken up by the arrival of the adult guests who joined us for the evening, we started playing hide-and-seek. The garden, with lots of bushes, log piles and compost bins, was good for the purpose, but the adjoining yard even better, with a variety of sheds and storage areas. My cousin Hans could not be found once. He had crept into the pigsty and hidden behind 'Fat Nellie', very much to the detriment of his white linen sailor suit.

We were made to wash our hands and tidy up in the wash house before meeting aunts, uncles and family friends for supper. This always consisted of potato salad and hot frankfurters, and beautifully garnished open sandwiches. There was a choice of black tea or beer for the adults and fruit juices for the children.

This being a special occasion and during holiday time, we were allowed to stay up and out much longer than usual, which was a treat in itself. As dusk fell, the garden was lit with Chinese lanterns, suspended in the trees. Magic! More music was played. Some people danced on the lawn. Father might be persuaded to sing for us or entertain us with one of his ditties, for all to join in with. A lot of laughter resounded through the evening. All passed far too soon.

At the end of the evening, the young guests were each given one of the tree lanterns, hooked on a wooden stick, to light their way home when they left with their parents, well beyond their usual bedtime. I have had many birthdays since, good parties too, but nothing could ever equal these feasts in the garden.

Rosemarie and Werner, 1930

Karlheinz, born 1936

Family portrait, 1 January 1944

Lauban in the early 1930s
Car rally with Albrechts

Seasonal Treats

During my childhood the years passed in a somewhat predictable way, each season with its own events, some of which affected Father's baking routines as well.

Nowadays, squirrels scuttling about on the damp lawn, making holes to bury their acorns and other collected treasures, bring back memories of the collecting fever, which governed our childhood pursuits throughout the year. There was not a path, woodland or riverbank within reach of home that we did not explore to discover and harvest nature's bounty. We knew where the first wild anemones flowered, where to find the yellow heads of *huflattich* in March – to be dried and added to Mother's herb collection as a remedy for chesty colds.

Fresh watercress was delicious on bread and butter, even if it meant acquiring soggy feet from stepping into the sodden meadows where it grew.

There would be wild strawberries in the disused quarry in June, and later, small but fragrant raspberries. Having to pick our daily quota of redcurrants on our plantation in July and August before being allowed to play out, swim or explore, was not half as exciting as discovering new patches of bilberries or blackberries, which stained hands and mouths – and clothes as well, to Mother's despair in the days before biological washing powders.

Even Father began to suffer from the collecting bug when the mushroom season got under way in August and September. There were huge stretches of pinewoods in the area, the ancient trees reaching skyward. Occasionally, sunrays penetrated their dark crowns to make patterns of light on the thick, bouncy needle carpet underneath. On the edge of this forest, colonies of bright yellow chanterelles might be found, a delicacy to be fried in butter and sprinkled with parsley from the garden. However, it was in the dark shady depths where Father's favourite fungi grew: *steinpilze* ('stone mushrooms') brown-capped, thick stemmed, firm-fleshed and rare. We children would have been happy enough to fill our baskets with more common but still edible fungi, which Father disregarded and left standing as unworthy of the effort to harvest them. Only his coveted prize specimens would do. These were later sliced and strung up for drying to be used as exotic flavouring for pâtés, soups and stews.

During the war we could earn a few pennies from a dealer for collecting sackfuls of acorns or horse chestnuts – to be converted into animal fodder.

Cranberries were best picked after the first frost. It was supposed to make them sweeter and improve their flavour. This was also a good time to pick up pinecones, ready to be painted or sprayed for Christmas tree decorations.

Snowfalls put an end to our explorations, but it would not be long before the first catkins appeared and nature once again invited discovery.

In the bakery, the customers expected their freshly made doughnuts on New Year's Eve and well into January. I loved to watch them being made. Lard and some sort of plant fat called palmin were heated in a shallow pan, large enough to hold fifty or sixty doughnuts at any one time. When bubbles formed on the side of a wooden stick dipped into the fat, it was hot enough to start baking. The yeast dough dumplings, about three inches in diameter, were gently placed into the seething fat, where they tended to drop to the bottom first before rapidly expanding to more than double their original size as the yeast did its work. They rose to the surface while growing, smooth, rounded mounds of still white dough. It did not take long for the half that remained submersed in the fat to turn a golden brown. With a spatula they were then flipped over to brown the rest of the dough. They were then lifted out of the pan with a perforated ladle and rolled in granulated sugar before being cooled on racks. People who did not like sugary fingers could have their doughnuts glazed with water icing. We had a little hand turned machine used to inject dollops of *Pflaumenmus*, a plum curd, into the middle of the confectionery before they cooled completely. They sold like hot cakes – giving us a productive end to the old year.

I don't remember anyone toasting the New Year in with

champagne. Mulled wine or 'grog', rum with hot water, were the drinks of choice to see the New Year in. When we were old enough to participate in the Silvester fun, we drank children's *Gluhwein*, hot raspberry cordial.

Silvester was a time for predicting what the New Year would bring. *Blei-giessen* was popular: little nuggets of metal were melted on a spoon over a candle flame, and the liquefied *blei* was poured into a pan of cold water, where it solidified into weird shapes. It required a lot of imagination to interpret these blobs as tangible objects, but some folks believed they saw wedding rings, cradles or money in them.

Just before midnight, we went outside into the cold to hear the church bells from Lauban ring the New Year in and fanfares sounding from the town hall tower.

January was the month for slaughtering one-year-old pigs. The country pubs staged *Wellfleischessen* feasts. Parts of the pigs were boiled in big kettles along with newly made liver sausage and *blutwurst*, a kind of black pudding, then served with sauerkraut, horseradish and mustard, using chunks of rye bread to soak up the flavoursome boiling liquid. *Korn*, a German type of vodka, went well with this. Such foods and drinks were certainly warming when temperatures outside might reach -20 °C.

A local chocolatier took advantage of the prevailing interest with pig slaughtering and displayed an almost full-sized pig in the window, made of marzipan and chocolate, and resting on a huge marble platter. Not only was it sensational to look at, we could go into the shop and buy pieces of 'pork', which would be skilfully sliced from the carcass, showing layers of marzipan interlaced with chocolate in thicknesses which varied according to the part of the animal they came from. I liked the streaky bits best, with fat and lean pork (marzipan and chocolate in more or less equal proportions). This shop also sold proper coffee, freshly roasted and ground, a luxury which Mother permitted herself from time to time. The pretty little caddies with English tea, which cost a lot of money, intrigued me.

The carnival season was not celebrated in the grand manner as they did in the Rhineland or Munich, but there were plenty of opportunities for people to let their hair down. I was fascinated by the adverts in the local paper, inviting people to costumed events and masked balls in some of the restaurants, which also had dance halls. However, I was far too young then to join in such fun.

Sobriety returned with Ash Wednesday, when Father produced *Schaumbrezel*, pretzels made from non-fat dough, which were part-cooked in boiling water, then hung up to dry on what I thought were clothes lines. When dry they were put into the oven to crisp up and brown a little. Although quite bland they were in great demand.

On *Gründonnerstag*, Maundy Thursday, we were allowed to go out begging for alms. I still don't know for sure what this custom was based on, but we thought it was fun knocking on friends' and neighbours' doors, asking for gifts. We went home with little linen sacks filled with plain small cakes probably bought at our shop, sugar or chocolate Easter eggs, or coloured or painted hen's eggs. Frau Hoffmann once dropped a fresh hen's egg into my bag instead of the hard-boiled one she had intended to give me. I cried my heart out when I saw the sticky mess it created.

We always had to search for Easter eggs in the garden on Easter Sunday, and had chicken for lunch and an Easter loaf with lemon icing at coffee time.

At Whitsun, we decorated our front door with fresh birch branches or even a small birch tree. They grew in profusion in the area, but one time we found that the pale green, delicate leaves had all gone – devoured by a plague of inch-long May bugs. When we got a chance we actually collected these huge beetles for a farmer who fed his livestock with them.

When the berry season started, Father began his mass production of shortbread flans to be filled with strawberries, raspberries, juicy morello cherries or even blueberries. They were all finished with a jelly topping. The stuff Mother used was 'Pomesin'. I liked the word – I even called one of my dolls Pomesina. It thickened fruit juice almost instantly and provided a perfect finish to the berry laden flans. We did not seem to be able to produce enough of them, especially when it was our turn to have a stall at the local *Schützenfest*, the grand annual event of the rifle club, when the best shot of the year was chosen in competition. The whole village took part in it.

The feast lasted four days and started with a torchlight procession and ended with a *Katerfrühstück*, a sour herring breakfast for those who had overindulged in food and drink during the celebrations. Children were well catered for during these days, with a splendid old-fashioned carousel with horses and moon swings (crescent-shaped boats, which rocked as the carousel moved). There was a clown to entertain us from time to time. What I liked best was Uncle Otto's gambling den. Actually, his mini casino consisted only of a beach umbrella and a table underneath, but what tense moments did we spend there, hoping to win a game! The table was divided into six fields, each one showing the picture of an animal. Bets of five pfennig (then about one penny) were accepted and placed on a chosen field. A huge dice, painted with horses, pigs, cocks, etc, identical to the ones on the table, decided the winner. All eyes were glued to this cube as it rocked and rattled down what looked like a tiny spiral staircase to eventually come to rest. If the picture on top tallied with the one we had placed our bet on, we became the proud winners of the colossal sum of twenty-five pfennig. Needless to say, it did not take long before such riches were spent on fizzy drinks, ice cream or another ride on the carousel.

The swimming bath opened in mid May and remained a popular meeting place all summer, not just for swimming and other water sports, but also for socialising and general relaxation for the whole family.

Around Michaelmas the season of *Gänsebratenessen* started in the local hostelries and in the country inns. Young geese were at their most succulent then and provided gourmet meals, served with red cabbage and cooked with wine apples and cloves. I liked the crackly skin best. This time was an opportunity for my parents to make the rounds of their country customers, enjoying their hospitality.

Little time was available for socialising when Christmas approached. Every day was busy in the bakery, but in December, the pace heated up and there was never an idle moment.

Advent in Silesia

As children, we never saw Father Christmas alight from a reindeer-drawn sledge in the middle of town or reside in a grotto for that matter, but when the nights drew in, and it began to snow, and when Mother got out her little brown ledger, we knew that Christmas could not be far away.

It was always preceded by weeks of hyper-activity since the bakery not only produced the usual daily bread, but also turned into a communal bakehouse on festive occasions. Few villagers had stoves or ovens that could manage the required volume of special occasion baking – so everyone came to us for that purpose.

Needless to say, that entailed strict organisation on Mother's part since Father and his two assistants could not cope with more than just a few enthusiastic amateur bakers at any one time, and the loading capacity of the baking oven, efficient as it was, was limited. So from November onwards, bookings were accepted and the brown ledger filled up with strange sounding entries, like:

7 a.m. Frau Schmidt – 10 lbs of flour (two poppy seed loaves and small *stollen*)

7.30 a.m. Farmer Wehner – 25 lbs of dough (large *stollen* only)

8 a.m. Frau Menzel – 15 lbs of flour (medium *stollen* and two trays of *pfefferkuchen*)

And so it went on until every minute of every December working day had been predestined for action.

Some days nearer to Christmas were set aside for the finer confections, which were not as durable as the Christmas loaves of one kind or other, which seemed to improve with maturity. Some families had to have expanses of crumble, cheese and apple cake as well, maybe even chocolate or marble babas. Nobody appeared to count calories then!

Mother's temper never seemed to fray as she dealt efficiently with the customers in the shop or directed 'bookings' with their bags and bowls of ingredients or their troughs of ready-made dough to the bakehouse or, later, made complimentary remarks as they collected the finished products on large wooden boards or in laundry baskets.

The house was a hive of activity during these fast-flowing days, full of chat and banter, full of warmth and delicious scents of browning cakes, almonds, raisins, rum and lemon. Baking sheets and tins occupied all available surfaces, trestles and shelves. Sometimes we had to squeeze up the stairs past layers of mouth-watering concoctions that were left there to cool on wooden retractable racks.

In the kitchen it was Elfriede, our trusted home help, who ruled the roost before Christmas. Her main brief was to keep us children out of mischief, but she also took over some of Mother's usual tasks; supplying breakfast to the bakers at unearthly hours, and substantial hotpot meals during the day, while brewing endless pots of grain coffee – not only for the usual occupants of the house but also for some of the customers. Some of them came over faint in the heat of the bakehouse or just because the excitement of it all was too much for them.

When pressure really built up, Mother sent us next door to Tante Lene who always said that she was getting too old to help. Bur she did not need a lot of persuasion to come at Christmas time. She put on her metal rimmed glasses instead of her pince-nez, donned a voluminous flowered apron and got down to some serious kneading and rolling out, as yet another set of villagers arrived with their tin bath full of dough to be shaped into Christmas loaves (*stollen*) or poppy seed loaves, from which the rum-scented filling sometimes escaped and caused Father to swear under his breath as the gooey mass coagulated on the polished base of his stove.

It was amazing that things went as smoothly as they did most of the time. Still, there were odd problems, like folks getting their dates mixed up and arriving on the wrong day with mounds of fermenting dough, which then had to be put outside into the snow to stop the yeast from overdoing its work before a lull in the system could be utilised to bake an extra batch of goodies. At times, a commotion was caused when finished products got mixed up because a tin's label or wooden stick came adrift and the stray cake had to be matched up with labelled items through gauging surface texture or comparing the size of the raisins in order to restore it to its rightful owner.

Sometimes we were sent out to remind villagers to collect their finished bakes since they caused serious congestion. If we were lucky we might get a ride home on a sleigh or, as once happened, in Herr Müller's Hanomag, then the only car in the village. Being generally helpful in locating and carrying things for customers had its rewards, although Mother did not like it if ten-pfennig pieces were pressed into our sweaty hands or we were plied with toffees. Frau Müller gave us a beautiful advent calendar once that we used for some years after. Each day in December a window was opened, exposing a festive picture when the light shone through, until, on Christmas Eve, the stable door could be opened to show the Nativity scene in glorious technicolour. The calendar also reminded us not to forget to put a shoe or boot on to the windowsill on St Nicholas' Day, for the saint to leave a small gift for us. We made sure that a new candle was lit each Sunday on our Advent Wreath, while Mother made us practise Christmas carols.

In spite of all the hustle and bustle Father would find time late one afternoon to put on his long boots and his *Loden* coat, and take an axe to the nearby forest to cut our Christmas tree. It had been earmarked months before for us on one of the mushroom gathering expeditions, which usually ended up with a drink in the forester's cottage. Occasionally someone had got there before him and a lesser spruce specimen had to do. If it was not as symmetrical as it might have been, he would cut a branch off the bottom, fitting it into a hole in the stem at a strategic point to fill an unwanted gap in the greenery. The tree was kept outside in our empty stable till Christmas Eve, when it would be brought in, firmly wedged into a star-shaped base, but still bare of all adornments. It vanished behind the doors of the sitting room, which was closed on that day to all but Mother and Father.

By midday, the last loaves and cakes had been collected and the doorbell in the shop ceased to tinkle. The bakers stacked away the cleaned baking sheets and moulds, folded down the racks and trestles, and created clouds of flour dust as they swept the floors – till Frau Legner stopped them in their tracks and showed them how to work properly. She was a withered little woman with wispy hair and a careworn face, but could she scrub! Her sinewy arms moved the brush like lightning over the sticky boards and dough troughs in a spray of sand and lather. When she had finished the wood was almost white and the flour sieves, fat tubs and the terrazzo floor looked like new.

Nobody was allowed to touch Father's beloved baking oven. It was he who raked the embers in the grate and put just enough coal on to keep the oven warm for roasting our Christmas goose the next day. The enamel casing was buffed and the steam valves polished till they shone like Frau Legner's taps.

The house was strangely empty and quiet later. There was just the mysterious rustle of paper beyond the locked door and the clinking of pots and pans in the kitchen as Mother and Elfriede set about preparing the Christmas Eve meal, which was always a simple dish of potatoes, kale and fried sausages.

We had a bath in the zinc tub in the kitchen, and when we put on clean clothes and our woollen coats and hats to go to church, anticipation began to mount. What would the tree look like this year? And what presents would Father Christmas have spread on Father's writing desk, covered with a white linen cloth, rather than the usual knick-knacks, which we were not allowed to touch?

We walked to the church through the crunchy snow while the church bells rang and daylight faded away. At the sight of the first star the candles were lit on the tree in the church and the choir sang so sweetly that we could not help being strangely moved. Still, we were far too excited to listen to what the pastor had to say and could not get home quickly enough after the service.

We had to be patient a little longer. After our meal, Mother and Father put the finishing touches to whatever they were doing in the sitting room while we helped to wash up and tidy the kitchen.

We listened with trepidation to some knocks on the window and a gruff voice demanding to know if the children had been good enough to deserve presents. We never saw Father Christmas since, according to Mother, he had too many other houses to visit, but we did see the result of his call when the old brass bell sounded, Father began to play carols on the piano and, at long last, the door opened to reveal our Christmas tree and presents for all in full splendour.

Snow

We could not understand why Mother hated snow. She admitted that it looked pretty enough as it drifted down from feather bed clouds, smoothing out rough village streets and covering trees, pillars, poles and garden fences with fluffy mounds. But there the liking ended.

I suppose it had something to do with the fact that, until the snow had settled to form a solid sheet that would stay firm until the next snowfall or until it melted, she fought a losing battle to keep the tiled shop floor dry and safe. Every time a customer entered, clumps of snow were deposited on the terrazzo, and melted in the warmth that emanated from the bakehouse and spread through the building. The cast iron door scraper did not do much good, and the coconut mat near the door became a nuisance rather than a help as it became soggier with each foot that trod on it, oozing slushy rivulets.

So, when she was not serving customers or listening to the latest gossip and fearful predictions of avalanches or folks losing their way and freezing to death in the nearby mountains, she would mop the floor, drying it carefully with old towels for fear that someone might fall and sustain an injury. Fräulein Krause sprained her ankle once, but seemed to be more upset by dropping the gateau she was collecting for a birthday party. Anyway, the event had endless repercussions. Mother was blamed. It seemed unfair. What was Fräulein Krause doing walking about in high-heeled shoes in such weather, when everyone with any sense donned lace-up boots or wore galoshes over sturdy shoes? I don't think Wellingtons could be found locally then.

While Mother had this love/hate relationship with snow, I, along with my brother, cousins and friends could not get enough of it. Considerable creativity was displayed in making snow sculptures and snowmen of various shapes and sizes, with coal for eyes, carrots for noses and sometimes gherkins for ears. The postman thought Christa's 'Venus de Milo' was rather 'rude'. Snow huts were also popular, created either by making a large snow heap, patted down with shovels into a solid mass, which could be hollowed out, or by rolling snow into columns that were then piled on top of each other to form walls for supporting planks as a roof, with more snow on top. Some of these structures lasted for weeks.

The railway embankment behind the garden made an ideal slope for sledging. It was actually forbidden territory because of the *Bimmelbahn*, the local train, which chugged along from time to time, come snow or high water.

Outside the village, long, gently rising hills made ideal nursery slopes for first skiing efforts when we had graduated from our *schlitters*, small, shaped wooden boards with upturned toe ends strapped to our boots. They got us used to walking, sliding, balancing and turning on snow-covered surfaces.

Our skis were also of a rather primitive type, with webbing loops to slide our boots in. We would not have won any competitions with them but they gave us rudimentary skills in this sport and occupied us on many winter afternoons. We had no stylish ski trousers or waterproof anoraks, just fleecy training suits, which got damp eventually from falling and rolling in the snow, and from the sweat generated by the energetic exercise.

When we had had our fill of this, or when darkness fell mid-afternoon, we slid home satisfied and glowing. We had to shed our damp clothes in the wash house, before being allowed inside the kitchen or the sitting room. Grain coffee and crisp rolls made welcome refreshments for us, while our wet outfits were draped over rails near the baking oven to be dried for another day's activities.

Trains and Travels

I rarely travel on trains these days, but they have played a significant part in my life, taking me to exotic places, taking me away
from danger, occasionally changing the course of my life.
Certainly, myriad fond and sad memories are associated with
trains and railways from childhood onwards. I could not imagine
my early years without them.

While many of the village women worked for one of the
handkerchief manufacturers in Lauban, a high percentage of men
were employed in the *Reichsbahnausbesserungswerk*, the regional
centre for maintenance and repair of the rail network, and the
passenger and goods trains that used it.

Most of our neighbours worked there and lived in flats provided by the company, including Uncle Max, the husband of one
of my father's sisters.

They did not seem to have a works canteen. The men provided their own lunchtime snacks, or what was very popular, had
their midday meal delivered to them by their womenfolk in
lidded enamel boxes and cans, and screw-topped tin flasks before
vacuum flask became fashionable and Tupperware was invented.

Children were actually not allowed on to the premises, but
occasionally Tante Lene would allow us to accompany her on the
'soup run' and persuade Uncle Max to let us peep into the huge
work halls where large engines towered over us and men worked
on them – scraping, soldering, greasing and buffing.

Little flat trucks stood in one corner, ready to be taken out to
run along and inspect the rail-tracks, junctions and signals,
tightening screws and repairing any damage that could be rectified
on site.

Most of the engines were modern electric ones, but steam
engines were still in use in places. There were huge coal heaps in
the sidings, ready to fill up the tenders before the finished engines
steamed out again into circulation. Shunting never ceased. One

could not escape the sound of clanking metal, the hissing and huffing of steam as it began to turn the wheels, and the warning whistles which sounded – all very exciting, even awe-inspiring, when experienced at close quarters by diminutive onlookers.

These monsters were part of the bigger world in which to us Berlin, Breslau, Dresden and Leipzig were quite faraway places.

Our little local train was rather less daunting; yellow, neat and clean, since, being electrically powered, coal and steam never touched it. Childhood days were punctuated by the tinkle of its bell as it passed on the embankment at the back of our garden every hour. You could set your clock by it.

It came from the main station in Lauban, a mile or so away, and had just reached full speed when the 'bim-bim-bim' sounds announced that it was approaching the first stop near us.

A brief halt and then the *Bimmelbahn* took off again, past the swimming baths, the basalt quarry and the brickworks, to the next village.

We would travel there when visiting friends or going to a garden restaurant for coffee and cakes on a Sunday afternoon. There were swings and little carousels to amuse us children while the adults gossiped with friends.

Steinkirch, the next station, bordered on a large forest, popular for berry and mushroom gatherers. My godfather, Uncle Kruger, lived in Beerberg, the last station before the terminal near the Czech border.

He and his family lived in a somewhat dilapidated mansion, which apparently had been bought cheaply at the height of inflation in the 1920s, allegedly with some gold he had inherited. He did not work on a regular basis nor pay much attention to house maintenance, but was an inventor.

One of the ramshackle but spacious outbuildings was his workshop, where dangerous looking machines stood in foot-deep sawdust and all manner of tools littered the surfaces. An obsolete threshing machine rotted away in a corner, and the high rafters harboured owls and bats.

One summer, Uncle Kruger was building egg laying boxes – little wooden houses into which a hen was placed. The weight of a newly laid egg released a small lever, which opened the box to allow the hen to escape when it had done its duty. I was allowed to help at the time, assembling structures and knocking nails into planks.

His egg laying boxes did not seem to be the great success he had expected them to be, so Tante Kruger and daughter Margot had to supplement the family income by taking in paying guests. These people came in the summer months to relax in the parklands, bathe in the river or explore the forelands of the Sudeten Mountains with their wooded dells, old castle ruins, rivers and lakes.

Since I knew the environment reasonably well I acted as guide at times, pointing out the secret path to the one hundred steps that led up to the top of a big reservoir, which supplied water to the area and fed an electric generator plant. Occasionally the huge dam of the reservoir overflowed, when thunderstorms in the mountains unleashed cloudbursts of some magnitude. We always ended up on the terrace of the Lake Hotel, where the most delicious ice cream could be bought.

Another tour was to Lauban on the *Bimmelbahn*. The visitors never seemed to tire of inspecting the medieval town walls and guard towers and the colonnades of the cobbled market place. Refreshments in our garden usually ended the day before the guests returned to the Kruger Mansion on the little yellow train.

The Kruger guests usually came from Berlin, as indeed did a number of other visitors, including my Uncle Bruno, who used to spend a few summer weeks with us every year – his *Sommerfrische*, as he called it. I suppose the area had a lot to offer to town dwellers who craved fresh air and relaxation as well as gentle diversions like sightseeing, rambling, bathing and sampling the delights of country inns and garden restaurants.

Village folk on the whole did not travel a great deal. If someone had been on the express trains, going to weddings, funerals or other family occasions, it was big news and avidly discussed in the shop, which acted as a kind of news agency and centre for gossip.

The railway families went away sometimes with their free travel vouchers. Some of them had ventured as far as the Baltic Sea, where there were some holiday homes for railway employees. Hans and Christa, my cousins, and their parents went to the Isle of Rügen and made us envious with their tales of chalk cliffs, high waves and beaches with *Strandkörbe*, hooded wicker beach chairs on swivel bases, which could turn towards the sun or away from the wind. If one was lucky, pieces of amber could be found on the sands.

The only person who regularly travelled abroad was Frau Menzel, the wife of a local spirit and liqueur manufacturer. She lived on the edge of the village in a splendid villa and was the only local woman who could drive a car when her chauffeur was otherwise engaged. She was like an exotic bird when she floated through the village in her Parisian finery – somewhat out of place among the down-to-earth villagers. She certainly provided plenty of material for gossip and a degree of envy. According to the housekeeper she wandered through the blue, green and yellow rooms of her house in the nude and had been seen sunbathing naked in the garden behind a palisade. She spent the 'season' in Dresden or Berlin, going to the opera, concerts and exhibitions with her arty friends who occasionally drove through the village in their fancy sports cars.

In the mid 1930s the government launched a new scheme, *Kraft durch Freude* (strength through joy), to give the working population a chance to take holidays at a reasonable cost in the more touristy parts of the country, like the Alps, or even in selected places abroad. Father took advantage of this offer. He travelled by express train to Hamburg, where he boarded the St Louis, a big new passenger liner, for a cruise through the English Channel and across the Atlantic to Madeira.

We never heard the last of it, especially the story of the storm in the Gulf of Biscay when all the holidaying passengers and even some of the crew were sick, and he was the only one to turn up for breakfast. The captain asked him to his table. As compensation for the rest of the family, Mother took us to Spindelmühle, a resort in the Sudeten Mountains, where she had spent some time working before her marriage. We were utterly spoiled by her former employers and stayed in a very smart hotel with a balcony, overlooking the majestic mountains.

My first big chance to travel some distance came when I was eleven. Uncle Bruno and Tante Lieschen invited me to Berlin.

Mother had some misgivings at first but was eventually persuaded that I was capable of using the through-train alone, providing that I was collected at my destination. Oh, the excitement of it all! I remember wearing a newly-made brown and beige pepita coat and a matching hat to impress Tante Lieschen, who was a very smart lady.

Mother had made a lovely strawberry flan, for me to take to Berlin – Uncle's favourite cake. It was carefully placed on top of my suitcase on the luggage rack in its presentation box, but unfortunately it slipped off in Cottbus, when a new engine was attached to the train. Still, my relatives did not seem to worry much about the spoiled contours of the flan, which were eventually camouflaged with mounds of vanilla flavoured whipped cream.

I had been afraid that I might get lost in the crowds who alighted at the *Ostbahnhof*, a vast station with many platforms and a huge glass domed roof, and was glad to see familiar faces. In no time I was bundled into a taxi, bemused and bewildered by the vastness and strangeness of the environment I found myself in.

Everything was huge and overwhelming: the tall business houses and department stores on the way, massive churches and palaces which flanked the wide avenue we travelled on towards the Brandenburg Gate, which I had seen on pictures before. There were trams and buses and more people than I had ever seen in one place before.

It was almost an anticlimax when the taxi turned into a quieter side street towards the Remmler factory and its fancy entrance gate. Uncle Bruno was the resident housemaster there.

He seemed to do a multitude of jobs in this pharmaceutical firm, acting as receptionist and security guard in the entrance lodge, which was also his office where he received orders and made sure goods were dispatched. From there he also directed the cleaning and maintenance staff and answered calls for help from the laboratories. In the meantime Tante Lieschen lounged about in her first-floor luxury flat, which not only had a balcony overlooking the tree lined avenue, but had a shower room as well as a bathroom, with chrome and glass fittings, like in a film set.

Uncle liked me to keep him company in the mornings. I was allowed to do some work in the office for him, like writing out labels for parcels to be dispatched, or sorting papers for filing, or making coffee for visiting salesmen. At lunchtime, some of the chemists came to the lodge to have their rolls and grain coffee and discuss the news of the day. They were obviously on very good terms with my uncle. Occasionally they sent me across the road to the pub to buy bottles of beer or frankfurters with mustard on little cardboard trays. They seemed to enjoy giving me tips for my errands – useful spending money.

Tante Lieschen appeared later in the day to take me out, giving me a taste of city life and every conceivable mode of transport. I had never been on a tram before and loved the way they tinkled along the route, metal wheels grating on metal tracks, causing sparks to fly at times.

Even more exciting were the underground trains; the U-Bahn and its underground stations with shops and cafes. I had to sit tight or cling to a support pole, because the trains moved very fast. Sometimes the U-Bahn surfaced, and we had glimpses of canals, bridges and stately buildings before vanishing underground again.

Another first encounter for me was with an escalator, or 'rolling stairs' as we called them. Most of the massive department stores had them. These places sold everything, including the latest fashion items, which at the time seemed to be transparent plastic raincoats with matching umbrellas in pastel shades. I would have loved to have a pale blue one, but they were not available in my size and, in any case, would have made a vast hole in my spending money.

It felt good, doing some of my own shopping. I especially liked the automatic restaurant where one could buy snacks, drinks and ice lollies from little drawers once coins had been put into a slot. Tante Lieschen bought me a red patent leather handbag, which I treasured for years to come.

Since my relatives had no children of their own, they spoiled me thoroughly and made me feel quite grown-up when I was allowed to accompany them in the evening for meals in garden restaurants with lamps on the tables and accordion players. The highlight of my two-week stay was a boat trip on one of the vast lakes near the town, ending with viewing a spectacular fireworks display at Treptow Bridge.

I can't remember a great deal about my home journey except that my head was spinning with new impressions. What I do remember well is that friends and classmates envied me for a long time to come.

Health Matters

I still bear the marks of my first smallpox vaccination, four notable scars on my right upper arm, inflicted on me when I was just a few weeks old. The procedure was compulsory then. A reinforcing vaccination was done before we left school at fourteen but this time only one pustule was raised, which we bore like marks of achievement, comparing the size of our blisters and walking around with a white armband for a few days, warning people not to touch us.

There were no other immunisations then, so it was left to nature whether we got away lightly or succumbed to one of the epidemics of infectious diseases that regularly threatened the child population and gave rise to a lot of scaremongering and speculations in the shop.

Chickenpox, mumps, measles, rubella and even whooping cough were generally seen to be almost inevitable and more of a nuisance rather than truly serious afflictions, although there were, of course, occasional complications.

Diphtheria and poliomyelitis were the diseases that really worried everyone, since they inevitably brought about a number of fatalities and permanent disabilities. News of an outbreak of either of these in the area sent shock waves through the village and set the school on red alert. The teachers made us bring mugs and little bottles of hydrogen peroxide to school, which we diluted and gargled with at the beginning and the end of the school day – in an attempt to kill nasty germs that might be harboured in our tonsils and could be breathed out over our friends.

I don't actually recall a single case of diphtheria or polio in the village during my school days, while tales of afflicted children elsewhere during the epidemics, usually in late summer, were rife. Death tolls were given in the daily papers and there were repeated reports of children having to have their throats cut open to insert a breathing tube when the diphtheria membrane threatened to choke them to death. Polio could also stop sufferers from breathing when the chest muscles were paralysed. The only way to save the patients was to put them into an iron lung (a kind of pressure chamber).

The most serious infection I had was scarlet fever, now easily treatable with antibiotics. It occurred in a rather virulent form in the 1930s.

I had had a sore throat for a day or so but was determined not to miss a mushroom picking expedition with Father. By the end of the afternoon I was hot and flushed, and felt so dizzy that Father had difficulties in transporting me home on his bike. I was incapable of riding mine.

The district nurse happened to be in the shop when we reached home and looked at me with professional interest, recognising some of the typical signs of scarlet fever, including a 'strawberry tongue' and 'circum-oral pallor', a strange pale area around the mouth while the rest of the face was scarlet. An ambulance was called immediately because I could not be left in an environment where food was being prepared and sold. I was past caring what happened to me then. Mother cried when I was carried out on a stretcher.

The first few days in the isolation ward of the fever hospital passed in a haze of delirium and semi-comatose oblivion. Eating was impossible, drinking very difficult, I felt sick and I gagged when efforts were made to obtain throat swabs, not so much to verify that I had scarlet fever but to exclude the possibility of diphtheria. Luckily no organisms of that kind were found, but I was nevertheless seriously ill for about ten days and had turned from a chubby nine-year-old into a scraggy near-skeleton. When I was allowed to get up to the bathroom for the first time a couple of weeks later, I just flopped on to the floor.

I shared a room with my aunt and Elfriede, our mother's help, who had both also contracted the disease. They were not as seriously affected in the acute phase of the illness but suffered heart and kidney complications later, which was not uncommon.

Visitors were barred from the isolation ward, but we did see family members and friends through the double-glazed windows at specific times and were thoroughly spoiled by the cards, poems and gifts they brought to cheer us up. We were sorry for Sister Gertrud, the nun who was in charge of the ward with very little help, when yet another basket of fruit or yet more tins of cake were left at the outer door to be given to us. Our room was at the end of a long corridor.

Gradually my strength returned and my hands and feet began to peel – a process which needed to be complete before I was declared infection-free and ready to go home, about six weeks after my admission.

Everything I had been wearing or using in hospital was left behind to be destroyed when I entered the checkout bathroom eventually for a final disinfectant wash. New clothes awaited me at the exit door. I had not expected to feel as weak and frail as I did when exposed to the fresh, late October air and had to walk one hundred yards or so to the waiting taxi.

It took two more weeks before I was back at school. I had missed the potato harvest holidays, and the usual autumn fun of gathering acorns and conkers.

Later that year, Mother suffered from gallstones. She would not easily give in to the severe colicky pains she had at times, but saw our family doctor eventually. He advocated an operation, but had no objections to Mother trying out an unconventional treatment with a 'patent cure' first, which one of her customers swore by. She knew several people whom it had helped.

It entailed starving for a day or two, and then taking a dozen vile-tasting oil capsules on which Mother nearly choked.

She felt dreadful after that, sick and unable to work, which was indeed worrying. However, after forty-eight hours of agony, everything calmed down. She felt like eating, and her gallstones appeared to have vanished and caused no further problems.

Helpful as the advice on a 'patent cure' had been this time, other recommendations by the same person almost led to disaster.

Mother had always used common sense in feeding her off-spring, but when my younger brother was born and breastfeeding no longer sufficed, she took Frau Remple's advice and sent off for Pauli's Nahrspeise. It was supposed to be particularly nutritious and certainly helped the baby to put weight on rapidly, but it obviously lacked some essential nutrients. By the time my brother was one year old he looked a sorry sight, with bleeding gums and bruises like a battered baby – in fact he had scurvy, a vitamin C deficiency syndrome. Luckily, this could be rectified, and there were no long-term problems. For many years after that no major health issues arose, once the usual childhood infections had been overcome.

There were some minor indispositions which Mother cured using tried and tested home remedies:

Coughs and colds were soothed with *huflattich* tea (coltsfoot), honey and, if necessary, steam inhalations.

Linseed poultices dealt with earaches.

Halswickel were effective for sore throats. A fold of flannel was soaked in cold water and draped round the neck, then covered with a woollen sock. It seemed to take the heat out of the inflammation and eased breathing as the water moistened the air through evaporating.

Indigestion and other tummy aches got the peppermint treatment, the herb being grown and harvested in the garden. Vile-tasting *wermut* (vermouth) infusions were used occasionally.

Lime blossom, camomile and valerian infusions cured myriad little aches and pains, and sleeplessness too.

Burns and scrapes were painted with the juice of aloe vera leaves or calendula butter.

Dr Fraenkel, our family doctor, did not acquire riches through us, but took an avuncular interest in the family. Unfortunately he was dead by the time I was fourteen and could have done with his knowledge and expertise in dealing with my broken ankle. He had been told that, being a Jew he was no longer allowed to practise. He poisoned his wife and shot himself.

Part Three

War, and an Uneasy Peace

The Beginning of the War

1 September 1939

'You'd better go now to collect the bucket pump from the council office,' Mother said when I entered the shop, having spent one of my last vacation days with a friend.

The place was buzzing with voices, quite unusual for a week-day mid-morning in the baker's shop, when most customers had already bought their daily bread and roll supplies. I wondered what had happened to cause the excitement and Mother's strange request. I must have looked perplexed, since everyone wanted to tell me the latest news all at once.

'It's war.'

'German troops went into Poland this morning.'

'We might be bombed.'

There had been some talk about air raid precautions in the village some months ago, and rather officious representatives of the council had instructed people about converting cellars into air raid shelters, putting containers with sand into the attics should they be needed to smother flames, and how to use bucket pumps to deal with stray incendiary devices.

Nobody took this very seriously at the time, since no one believed that war could possibly happen to disturb the rural peace. In the event, Frau Grabs, the village gossip and pessimist, was right for once and, after uttering what amounted to 'I told you so', went home to stack another sandbag against her cellar window.

Eventually the upset shoppers scattered, clutching extra loaves of bread and bags of flour in their arms in case of shortages and emergencies.

I joined the queue at the council depot to claim our makeshift fire extinguisher, which we had ordered months earlier, but had failed to collect so far.

Later that day, when folks were trying to black out their windows and the glass panes in doors with black paper, blankets or, in a few cases, proper blackout shutters, a siren began to howl. I had heard it only once before, when the flour mill caught fire. Then and now it really chilled the blood.

Strangely enough, instead of the eerie sound sending everyone to their improvised air raid cellars, the village street filled with people who gawped skyward to see if they could spot the oncoming invaders of their peace. They did not seem to be aware of possible dangers to life and property, but felt the need to seek the comfort and company of others rather than to segregate themselves in their lonely cellars.

It was just as well that no bombing or shooting took place; indeed, there had been no danger at all. The sounding of the siren had just been a practice run by Herr Huber, who had custody of this instrument, as well as being the local gravedigger and nightwatchman, and now also the person who made sure that blackout dictates were adhered to.

The first days of September 1939 were punctuated by fanfares sounding from the wireless, which announced the latest advances of the German troops in Poland, and also the news that England had declared war on Germany, the significance of which passed us by at the time.

Although there was a great deal of discussion going on in the shop at first, and the usual gloom and doom predictions by Frau Grabs, everyone was cheered by the rapid end to the Polish invasion. All was quiet on the Eastern Front by the end of September. Still, hopes for an early end to the war faded as the months passed – in fact, war dragged on far longer than anyone had anticipated, but as children, we were barely aware of its progress.

Holland, Belgium and France were occupied by German forces comparatively quickly. Once again the fanfares blared when the British troops withdrew from France at Dunkirk and when Paris was overrun.

There was some concern when Hitler turned against Russia, which till then had been a so-called ally. But even here early advances by the German force meant that not only the Western Front but also the Eastern Front were far away enough to be easily ignored by someone who had not been personally affected by tragedy. It did not seem possible that village life would ever substantially change in this sheltered backwater, where till 1945 not a single bomb had fallen, although over-flying aircraft occasionally caused the siren to howl.

Of course, the absence of men drafted into the army, and particularly those who were killed in action or declared missing, had great impact on some families. Women had to assume responsibilities for families, homes, farms and businesses, but there was also a lot of camaraderie and support on offer. The promise of better things to come sustained everyone. There was no real hardship in daily living.

Food rations were augmented by intense cultivation of gardens and allotments, which also made room for an increasing number of hen houses and rabbit hutches.

It was a matter of honour not to waste anything. What could be recycled in any way was collected: bones, paper, metal of any kind, including toothpaste tubes. We also started a silkworm farm in one of the classrooms to aid the production of silk for parachutes. We soon got used to the creepy-crawlies on their trestles at the back of the room and watched with wonder how the skimpy little worms grew fat, greedily consuming the mulberry leaves which we took it in turns to collect from the newly planted hedges near the swimming pool. It was fascinating to see the worms begin to spin their webs, eventually surrounding themselves with a smooth, silky, white cocoon, as light as a feather. We no longer skied in winter, since clothing and equipment had been donated to the war effort in Russia. Somehow I could not imagine our primitive sports gear having much impact on the Russian army.

No one thought of wasting time and resources on arrangements for the usual annual village festivities, but on a smaller scale we still enjoyed life and the challenges of 'making do' with whatever was available, like converting flour sacks into children's pants and inventing recipes for artificial liver sausage, which included bread, onions, yeast and lashings of garlic and marjoram, as far as I can remember, which actually tasted very good.

Our childhood expeditions to explore the riches of fields and woodlands assumed more importance: berries, mushrooms, wild sorrel and watercress made tasty additions to rationed food. We competed in collecting grain and potatoes left behind when the harvesters had gone.

There was nothing to stop us from pursuing the games we usually played throughout the year – marbles, spinning tops, hula hoops and ball games had not lost their attractions The swimming bath continued to be a focal point in summer months. Not a day went by without meeting our friends there to socialise and pursue various forms of water sport: racing, diving, playing ball games or trying to dislodge competitors from floating beams.

Occasionally Frau Stefan, who dispensed *Ersatzkaffee* or luridly coloured soft drinks at the Strandcafe, asked if I could persuade Father to bake a batch of *Amerikaner* for a special occasion. These flat, iced sponge cakes were enjoyed by young and old alike.

The Strandbad in Kerzdorf, 1941

Village School

School, of course, proceeded as usual – from seven in the morning until midday on summer days and from eight until one in the afternoon in winter. The dashing headmaster of the village school went to the Western Front and was replaced by a wounded veteran of the First World War. His leg prosthesis creaked with every step he took. During particularly cold spells we were encouraged to bring a briquette to school with us to feed the tiled stove, the only form of heating in the classroom. The large spaces were difficult to keep warm, but I can't remember feeling any particular hardship as a result.

Fräulein Kunze was the mainstay of the village school. Everyone in the village knew her. She seemed to have been around forever. Father and his contemporaries had been taught the three Rs by her, and I knew that Fräulein Kunze would take me under her wing when I started school at six.

She was a tall, slim woman of indeterminate age, her hair swept back into a firm bun at the nape of the neck. She looked quite severe, but laughter lines around the eyes and mouth indicated that she could see the funny side of things.

She was one of four teachers who staffed the village school, and was responsible for the younger end of the school population, which totalled no more than about 120 pupils aged from six to fourteen – the leaving age at the time.

The school year started at Easter. It was customary for parents to give school entrants a cornucopia filled with Easter eggs or other small gifts, to sweeten the transition to a more serious part of life. Fräulein Kunze made this rite of passage a really special occasion by staging a play, casting pupils who had just completed their first school year as Easter bunnies. They had to dress up for the part, and in the course of the entertainment presented the new students with the cornucopias to welcome them to her class. It definitely helped to break the ice and seemed to make the newcomers keen to get on with schooling so that they could become Easter bunnies the following year.

After this fun time the serious work began, just for two hours per day at first. Armed with our slate boards, slate pencils, colourful sponges and drying cloths, we sat on hard benches in straight lines and began to practise the art of writing, starting with making upward and downward strokes of a prescribed length and equally spaced. More advanced forms of writing were gradually introduced. My handwriting even now reflects the initial drill in Gothic script, which made a later transition to Latin lettering more difficult.

After a period of concentrated screeching of slate on slate we had a story read to us to whet our appetites for the time when we could read properly ourselves and could make up and write our own stories.

After a break and a run in the schoolyard, we were introduced to the mystery of sums and the rudiments of manipulating figures. Fräulein Kunze made a game of it, and I seem to have assimilated basic mathematics without any difficulties – even now I occasionally beat Carol from *Countdown* to the result of the mathematical game.

The two concentrated teaching hours passed quickly and in a very disciplined way. There was no playing about or wandering around the classroom, but none of us objected, and we looked forward to more of the same the next day.

The teacher was firm with us, but also fair. She showed no favouritism, nor belittled anyone who was slower in grasping the essentials of writing, reading or completing sums.

However, she was still very good at encouraging effort by praising individual improvements in performance. I can still hear her talking to my bench neighbour who found some task rather difficult to perform.

'This is a beautiful letter G, Peter, why don't you try to make the others look just as good?'

And he did – slowly but surely, his stuck out tongue indicating his concentrated effort.

There was no doubt that Fräulein Kunze could get the best out of her flock. By the time I was seven years old I wanted to be a teacher just like her.

Once basic skills had been taught and absorbed, more enter-taining activities were entered into, like singing and drawing and, a little later still, *Heimatkunde*, the study of our surroundings, which included some history, geography and botany, thus expanding our horizons and laying foundations for the later, more subject-orientated, school years.

Fräulein Kunze's dedication and enthusiasm for teaching and encouraging learning beyond the classroom was an inspiration to us. I can't think of anyone else who might have laid a better foundation for future studying, indeed, for life in general.

When I was ten, my compatriots and I became pupils in the senior school, just across the schoolyard, where the lessons were more subject-orientated.

There were no free state secondary schools in the area. Parents who could afford to do so would send their offspring to the Lyceum or the Gymnasium in Lauban. An alternative for higher education was the middle school in a neighbouring town, where technical subjects of a less academic nature were taught. It also had to be paid for, and meant a daily train journey of about ten miles each way.

My parents were not poor, but had little money to throw about, so none of these options applied to me. I myself was quite happy to stay at the *Volksschule*, which I loved to attend, along with all my friends. It was also within easy walking distance from home.

Looking back now, I realise how fortunate we were to be educated there by dedicated, imaginative and caring staff, who were known and well respected by all the villagers.

On the whole, the pupils did not appear to present too much of a challenge to them. The cane was used on some occasions when admonition and reasoning had no effect on cheekiness or other undesirable behaviour. Offenders who painted chalk graffiti on surfaces in the schoolyard were made to scrub them off with soap and water after school hours or at times when their friends went to the swimming baths or to the school garden, activities that we all were very fond of. If someone could not keep up with the required learning in the classroom, extra tuition was offered. These *Nachhilfestunden* were sometimes given by fellow pupils who had mastered the subject. If none of this help had the desired effect in a reasonable time, the slow learner was simply not allowed to advance to the next class. *Sitzenbleiben* was definitely something to be avoided if at all possible. The prospect of it often spurred lazy pupils on to work harder.

While I loved Fräulein Kunze and thrived in her care for the first four school years, I was glad enough to advance to the senior classes with their new challenges and new experiences. Apart from receiving a solid grounding in German grammar, spelling and composition, in arithmetic, history and the geography of the world, we also learned more practical things like needlework, household management, basic cookery and gardening. Drawing and music were also on the syllabus.

Sport was taken seriously. We played various ball games and had athletic competitions with neighbouring schools. To my regret I was never entered for the triathlon. I was good at sprinting and high jump but could not get the hang of throwing a ball at any distance. Still, I was a good swimmer, and even won a silver laurel wreath on one occasion. The head teacher took pride in ensuring that no child left the school without being a safe swimmer. During the summer months we watched the thermometer in the schoolyard avidly, because if it reached 25 °C by 11 a.m. further lessons were suspended in favour of a walk to the swimming pool. A little extra homework made up for lost teaching time.

Before Christmas each year we staged a show, with sketches, recitals and song and dance routines. Once we actually staged a proper play. I was cast as the 'Sleeping Beauty' and have never forgotten the embarrassment I felt when my cousin had to kiss me awake.

I was not sure what I wanted to do as school leaving age approached. My parents wanted me to stay at home. An extra pair of hands would always be useful in household and shop, but I could not see myself forever in such a position.

'I have had a letter from the Education Department,' Herr Kirsch, our limping headmaster, announced one day. 'I have been asked to put forward names of pupils who might benefit from higher education and who have potential to become teachers.' A special scheme had been initiated with a view to filling gaps created by the war in the teaching profession.

Three names were put forward after consulting other teachers and parents. I was pleased to be one of them, but there were still hurdles to be overcome before being offered this opportunity of a lifetime.

Fifty candidates, including me, were summoned to a week-long selection camp. We were accommodated in a rather splendid mansion-like hostel and exposed to a full programme of teaching, testing and recreational activities. Apart from the type of examinations that we had been accustomed to – like essay writing, dictation and sums – we were given batteries of short answer and intelligence tests that were not commonly in use in ordinary schools.

We were also taught some completely new subject matters, like English as a foreign language and advanced mathematics, and had to demonstrate subsequent understanding. I still remember discovering square roots, which I had never heard of before. They had nothing to do with gardening.

The days started with sporting activities – jogging and gymnastics – followed by showers before breakfast and mornings and afternoons brimful with activity. The days ended with social gatherings of all candidates and staff, even some outside guests who were not introduced to us. We had to provide the evening entertainment as individuals, in pairs or small groups.

Two girls from Bunzlau played a most delightful violin duet, while a third played the piano. There were impromptu sketches, vocal solos and quartets. All I could think of was giving a rendition of a comical poem in Silesian dialect, recounting what happened to Karle, who had too much to eat and drink at a local pig slaughtering event. He had nightmares and dreamt that a herd of pigs came down the chimney and started to discuss what they were going to do with him. It had always raised a laugh when I had been encouraged to recite it at home or at some party, but I had not expected to be applauded as much as I was by this discerning audience. Even the stern maths examiner chuckled.

Against my expectations, I eventually heard through the headmaster that I was considered to be a very suitable candidate and would be offered a place in one of the boarding colleges at the end of the school year. Tuition would be free, but my parents were expected to make a contribution to my upkeep, which they gladly promised. Some of the very reasonable sum was actually given back to me as pocket money.

So my early wish to become a teacher like Fräulein Kunze now had a chance to become reality. In September 1942, a new chapter of my life started.

First school day, 1934

The school door, 1984

Leaving the Village School

My school days at Kerzdorf ended at Easter 1942. I was looking forward to taking up my scholarship at the boarding college, but not till September of that year.

There was no shortage of things to do in the meantime, workers being on short supply everywhere. I was helping out in the shop and in the bakery, and did simple bookkeeping in Tante Hanne's Auto Workshop. Little private motoring was done at the time, but military vehicles needed spare parts to be supplied and repair jobs to be done. Uncle Rudolf had to get his hands greasy again and Tante Hanne left her luxury flat to run the office and was glad to pay me a few pfennigs to do a little work for her every week.

In June I helped some friends with haymaking. Farmer Ulrich and his elderly brother still mowed their large meadows with scythes – with sweeping rhythmic movements. It was left to the women and older children to spread the newly mown grass with wooden rakes and to turn it over at regular intervals, helping it to dry. At the end of the day we piled it into stacks to prevent dew or rain wetting the whole lot again. The next day, the spreading and turning continued till the hay was ready to be carted to the hayloft.

One evening I rode home on my bike, taking a shortcut on a rutted path through the fields when my front wheel got stuck and sent me flying over the handlebars. I ended up on the grass verge in a heap, with the bike on top of me in the middle of nowhere.

I had visions of swooning away with pain and thirst as the sun moved lower on the horizon, but then I managed to attract the attention of Stummy, the 'village idiot', who was wheeling his little wagon through the fields in search of herbs and other greenery for his pet rabbits. First he stared at me in disbelief. When he realised that I could not get up, he lifted the bike off my limbs and offered to wheel me home in his cart, a prospect I did not relish. Still, he understood that help was needed, and alerted one of the few motorists on the nearest road to my plight. Eventually I ended up in my aunt's car repair workshop, which was fairly close to the scene of the accident. They actually had a telephone there, and managed to call the only available doctor in town that evening.

Dr Schwarz was nearly eighty and somewhat unsteady on his feet. He had come out of retirement since medical personnel to care for the general population were scarce during the war years. There was no emergency department in Lauban, and broken limbs did not merit hospital admission. No X-rays were taken, not even when it transpired a week or so later that my ankle injury was more complex than he had thought. He hummed and hawed and eventually sent me home with my leg strapped into a full-length traction splint, which I later realised was totally inappropriate for that type of injury.

When Mother called him out again we heard that he had died.

The female doctor who eventually arrived told us bluntly that she would not take any responsibility for the state I was in, but would attempt some damage limitation.

The district nurse, a nun from the convent in Lauban, could not hide her dismay when she saw my swollen, misshapen and discoloured leg. She crossed herself and moved her lips in a silent prayer before she immersed my foot in a bucket filled with water, to which *Staufer* salt had been added. It was very painful to hang the leg down. It felt like a lead weight. Cold compresses with *Essigsaurer Tonerde* followed, with a more soothing effect. I dreaded the daily hydrotherapy, but it helped to stimulate the circulation and made it possible to begin to wriggle my toes again. Still – the weird shape remained and no amount of supportive bandages helped to put me on my feet again.

The customers in the shop were well informed about my predicament and offered various advice, but neither arnica tincture nor calendula ointment were of much use. Someone suggested a trip to a shepherd in a nearby heathland area. The old man had the reputation for being able to manipulate, break and set bones, skills learned through experience with his flock of sheep. Apparently he had eased Frau Rempel's backache and sorted out other folk's knees, shoulders and elbows.

I can't say that I liked the idea of this unconventional treatment option very much, but realised that anything that might help to put me on my feet again was worth trying.

So one hot July afternoon I was bundled into Herr Müller's old Hanomag car, its tank filled with black market petrol, and driven to the shepherd's cottage. I had to go without Mother, since two neighbours had begged to be able to go along to have their ailments attended to.

Once there, I sat on an ordinary kitchen chair with my foot on a piece of cloth draped over the shepherd's lap. His work worn hands were surprisingly gentle as he felt the contours of my limb and tried to assess what movement was possible. He was not a man of many words, but grunted: 'You should have come earlier. I suppose something can be done. It's going to hurt a bit.'

It certainly did. I tried not to scream but could not help tears running down my cheeks as he pulled and twisted my bones in various directions, causing awful grating and clicking noises.

'Just stand up now,' he said then, and I could actually stand and support my weight on the 'bad' leg for a painful minute. It seemed like a miracle. Then he spread some very tacky, tar-like ointment on to some linen strips and tied them round my foot and lower leg. He said it would ease the discomfort and help the bones, sinews and muscles to heal together again. I was instructed to wriggle my toes frequently, walk a little several times a day, and go swimming with the covering still glued to my foot. This covering would come off of its own accord after a couple of weeks. I followed his advice diligently, and noticed daily improvements in mobility. I used my good leg to travel on a scooter to the swimming baths at first, then graduated to my bike until walking became less painful.

Sohrau Years

I was still limping when the summons came to report to the boarding college in Sohrau, Upper Silesia, for which I had gained a scholarship at the earlier selection camp.

It was 1 September 1942, exactly three years after the war started, when this new episode of my life began – the beginning of what were to be five years of intensive study. The first thing was to catch up with the traditional grammar school syllabus to reach 'Abitur' standard – similar to A-levels in England. This was the prerequisite for teacher training. The last year would be solely devoted to the theory and practice of pedagogy. We did not know then that the course would never be completed.

Having always liked school, I was excited at the prospect of further study at minimal cost to my parents. Though somewhat apprehensive at leaving the comfort and predictability of home, I still welcomed new challenges.

The local train took me to Kohlfurt where I could board the long-distance express to the furthest end of Silesia, close to the Polish border. Private travel was discouraged in the middle of the war, unless it was for business or work purposes, or urgent family reasons like illness, weddings and funerals. Most express trains to the Eastern provinces carried military personnel, and had just one or two coaches attached for use by the general public.

I had been told that three other girls would join the train en route and was more than glad to recognise the trio, whom I had met at the selection camp a few months earlier, on the platform in Bunzlau. It was reassuring to face the long journey and to gain first impressions of our new environment together.

The college turned out to be a very modern Bauhaus style building with wide entrance steps leading to an unadorned but still impressive foyer, with wide staircases leading upwards on both sides. The left wing of the flat-roofed building contained the classrooms, teachers' offices and our study rooms, while the right wing was given over to domestic and dining areas on the ground floor, and dormitories, bathrooms and shower rooms upstairs. Later, we became acquainted with the large, lofty sports hall that was also used as dance hall, general meeting place and stage setting for theatrical and musical performances.

Some of the cellars had been purpose-built as air raid shelters. We only used them on one or two occasions when foreign aircraft passed overhead on the way to more important targets.

The college catered for ninety students in three year bands, age fourteen to sixteen. Ten of us shared a dormitory. Our belongings were stored in lockers along the corridors. We never knew when our form tutor would decide to inspect them, so it was wise to keep our apparel immaculately tidy and in neat piles to avoid her displeasure – displeasure that resulted in finding our stuff in a heap on a sheet on the floor.

We were not supposed to keep food of any kind in our lockers and had to declare cakes, biscuits and sweets sent by our doting parents with laundry parcels. They were stored in a cupboard in the domestic area where we had to ask for access. The supervisor, Fräulein Lubeck held the key. She was a stern looking woman who would not tolerate any nonsense, yet who nevertheless could burst into fits of giggles at times. I got to know her softer side when I was delegated to do kitchen duties when my leg injury stopped me from participating in any sporting activities that required nifty legwork. Peeling potatoes for over ninety meals was no joke, but earned me the odd extra bun from Fräulein Lubeck, who was not averse to a bit of gossip while we drank a cup of herbal tea or malted grain coffee. I think she felt like an outsider among the academic staff members.

Swimming had remained on my timetable all the time and gradually I was able to participate in other sports again. Great attention was given to maintaining physical fitness at the college.

Every school day followed a definite pattern. We had to get up at 6.30 a.m. Washing and dressing had to be fast and efficient – no button left undone or laces unfastened – to be ready for the daily assembly in the entrance hall. One of the tutors would greet us, give us a motto for the day, and make any necessary announcements – for instance, about visitors coming to the college, changes in the daily routine, special events coming up, and so on. At the beginning of the week a flag was raised outside, to be taken in on Friday evening.

Breakfast was ready at 7.15 a.m., just bread or a roll, with margarine or butter and jam of some kind. Our beds had to be made, and were inspected before lessons started at 8 a.m. We had five hours of academic studies per day, till 1.30 p.m., with just a thirty minute mid-morning break for a drink and a snack. Lunch was at 1.45 p.m., followed by a free period till 3.30 p.m., when we could rest in bed, sunbathe outside or go for a walk. Coffee and a bun or a piece of cake at 3.45 p.m. revived us for the afternoon work period, if sport was not on the timetable. Ten of us shared a study room to get on with our homework for that day, or any long-term assignments we had to complete. Those of us who played instruments had practice periods allocated to us during this time. Saturday mornings were devoted to art and needlework. We had to knit socks and mittens, and learned to darn and patch clothes, also to make simple garments, using a range of seaming and stitching techniques. I must have been one of the first to invent mini-nighties – my material did not stretch any further.

After supper, at 7 p.m., we had 'evening rounds' three times a week, for choir singing, story or play reading, or a discussion on a topical issue, raised by a student or tutor. Often our discussions continued and took a different slant in the shower room or when we were in bed, with lights off at 9 p.m.

We had more time to ourselves at the weekend and found plenty to occupy ourselves.

We could walk in the woods or swim or paddle in the local lake. A favourite place for sunbathing was a redundant shooting gallery behind the college sports ground. Because of its sandy base, we called it Brighton Beach, not knowing that the real Brighton has a shingled shoreline. On cold and dull days we went to the cinema and visited a little local cafe, where gateaux or other confectioner's luxuries were available for double bread coupons. As a baker's daughter I was never short of them, and could give others a treat.

I thoroughly enjoyed the academic work. The teachers seemed to have been hand–picked for their enthusiasm and skill to get the best out of their students.

I thought I had received an excellent education at the village school, but had not realised how much further our horizons could still be widened. Soon square roots were no longer an unknown quantity, and ancient history caught my imagination. After a year's English study, we were introduced to Shakespeare, and eventually gave a performance of *The Merry Wives of Windsor* to a local audience and invited guests from other colleges and the education hierarchy. Fräulein Schmidt, the director of the college, who also taught English, had written a modified script for this and we all had to use our imaginations to produce appropriate scenery and make our costumes. I was Mr Shallow, and managed to fashion a tall top hat from blackout paper to go with my dark attire. My mother was not very pleased that I had cut up my petticoat to make a ruched collar to go round my neck. The show was a great success as, indeed, were other dramatic or musical performances that were staged from time to time.

Shakespeare in Sohrau, The Merry Wives of Windsor, *March 1944*

Fräulein Stolze was a musical genius who inspired the choir to sing rousing choral works. She actually made me like piano playing, which, at home, was the accepted thing to do, but there I did it without real enthusiasm. Now I surprised myself by playing quite intricate solo pieces at one of the school concerts – without sheet music to look at. I earned myself an opera ticket with this, and went to see and hear Wagner's *Götterdämmerung* in the opera house in Kattowitz, the main town of the province. It seemed to go on for hours, but I loved every minute of this new experience – the rousing music, the amazing scenery with fire and cloud effects, and the grandeur of the theatre itself.

Once a term, those who lived within reasonable travelling distance were allowed to go home for a long weekend. The eight of us whose homes were too far away to make the journey worthwhile stayed behind at the college.

We actually enjoyed these breaks when no schoolwork was required and rules were markedly relaxed. To save on lighting, heating and constant checks on blackout facilities, we all moved into one dormitory. Fräulein Lubeck did not expect us for breakfast till 9 a.m., and gave us special treats – in fact, she excelled in providing culinary feasts free from the constraints of mass catering. She had a cousin who was a forester and able to procure things we had never tasted before, like wild boar and venison.

We were still supposed to be in bed in good time, but the lights were not switched off till 10 p.m., rather than the usual 9 p.m., and no one seemed to mind that we read or chatted after this, and had midnight feasts of morsels from Fräulein Lubeck's cupboard or goodies that had somehow escaped confiscation. We seemed to be forever eating.

It was on one of those late evenings that I learned all about the 'birds and bees', almost everything there is to know of human reproduction from conception to birth and after. Sex education was not the done thing at the time, and I am sure I was not the only fifteen-year-old who was quite ill-informed in these matters.

Anyway, we listened avidly to Ruth's explanations. Her sister had had a baby recently, and her brother-in-law, an enlightened doctor, had answered all her questions openly and honestly. We could have saved the science teacher's blushes when the repro-ductive system crept up on the science syllabus later. We then seemed to know more than she did.

These interludes, as well as weekends in youth hostels in the mountains of Upper Silesia, provided welcome respite from our hectic school life. We were barely aware that all this happened in the middle of the Second World War.

However, holiday periods in the second and third college year brought us back to reality. Travel for civilians became ever more difficult. The few trains available to us were overflowing with passengers. We were lucky to squeeze in and find standing space only along the corridor for hours on end. Once Hilde and Ruth were pushed through a window by helpful soldiers so as not to be left standing on the platform.

It was on one of these long journeys home that I met Otto: tall, blonde and handsome. We talked for hours in the blacked out corridor and could not learn enough about each other. When the heating failed after midnight he put his greatcoat round my shoulders and when I reached my destination, he kissed my hand and promised to keep in touch. I suppose it was the first time I truly fell in love.

He kept his word and over the next eighteen months he wrote long letters whenever he found a chance to do so. He sent pictures and poems and, being an idealist, talked about his dreams for the future, which included me. However, I never saw him again. He was drafted to an SS unit to guard Hitler's bunker in Berlin and was presumably killed when the Russians overran the capital.

When we returned to Sohrau after the Christmas holidays of 1944, war events were definitely more ominous than they had ever been. My parents would have preferred it if I had stayed at home rather than return to the college, which was so much nearer to the Russian front, although no active fighting, was taking place at the time. Everyone pretended all was fine, but as the days passed and the magic weapons, which Hitler had promised would end the war, did not materialise, worry began to creep in. Indeed, it was just the calm before the storm that we experienced then.

One night in the second half of January we saw the sky in the east glow red, and imagined or perhaps really heard the rumble of bombs or artillery fire. So it did not come as a surprise when Fräulein Schmidt announced during next morning's assembly that she had been told to evacuate the college, because a new Russian offensive had started in the Krakow area, barely two hours away by train. Inquiries at the railway station had been futile: transport for more than ninety people could not be guaranteed. Yet she felt we had to leave by any means available as soon as possible.

I still remember her tearful last words: "I am sorry I have failed you. From now on it's everyone for himself.'

There was no panic, but we did not need to be told twice to start packing and, in the absence of other options, to try to find a train or bus to anywhere, as long as it was away from the advancing front. Difficult choices had to be made as to what to take and what to leave behind. Most of our belongings – clothes, books, works of art and other accumulated little treasures were stored in the air raid cellars. We never retrieved them. Of course, ever optimistic, we dragged along still too many possessions, only to dump them along the way towards what, at the time, was considered to be safety.

Eight of us banded together, and were lucky to find a train at Sohrau. It had just been returned to the station after repair work and was still empty: locked and waiting for an engine to arrive. Hundreds of other people also waited on the platform and stormed the compartments when the carriages were opened.

It took more then twenty hours to reach Bunzlau, Kohlfurt, and then Lauban via a complicated route involving several train changes, and two hours spent in a siding while the station we had just passed was bombed.

I think my parents had almost abandoned hope of seeing me again. They were overjoyed when a rather bedraggled-looking version of their daughter arrived, and they did not mind at all that two room-mates accompanied me. These friends had been unable to make contact with their parents who lived nearer to the war zone, and had been advised to leave with us rather than face uncertainties in trying to reach their homes.

Sohrau College

Relaxing at 'Brighton', June 1943

Comings and Goings

In early February of 1945, refugee treks of horse-drawn wagons began to appear on our roads, moving laboriously westward, away from the Russian invasion that was beginning to gather momentum. Friends and relatives from Middle Silesia stopped over in the village on their way to what they considered to be safety. We only heard much later that some of them, including Aunt Thea and her three young children, had just reached Dresden when the infamous bombing raids took place, which not only killed many natives but thousands of refugees who sheltered there on their journey to the west.

We had not a great deal to fear from Russian planes since their air force was almost non-existent by then, but unease gave way to fear as the war machine rumbled on, and on clear nights, the eastern sky glowed red.

The largest local employer, the regional rail repair organisation, thought it prudent to offer their employees and their families the chance to board trains for Munich, where similar workshops existed and some accommodation could be offered. Other villagers departed of their own volition and in no time, the place began to resemble a ghost town.

It was then that Mother's resolve – to keep the family together at home – began to crumble. Father could not leave the area since he belonged to a local unit of the *Volkssturm*, the equivalent of the Territorial Army. While there were still some civilians around, he intended to supply them with bread.

When a railway official friend suggested that room might be found for Mother, my young brother Karlheinz, and me on the last evacuation train to leave the sidings behind our garden, it was decided that we should take this chance of escape.

It was not an ordinary train, but a repair unit, which had to be available for emergency work for as long as the lines were open and repairs to tracks and trains might be required. We were sad to leave Father behind, but were glad when the train moved off eventually in the middle of the night on 17 February 1945, to the accompaniment of artillery fire.

A couple of bunk beds had been crammed into the tail end of the coach, and mattresses had been laid over drawers and chests that held tools and screws and other repair gear. There was little space for personal luggage, but bread and non-perishable foods like rusks, donated by Father, were taken along.

My brother and I were allocated the kitchen area in the front of the coach as sleeping quarters. The wooden benches were too short to lie on, so we slept on the floor on layers of cardboard, covered with a blanket. The tiny Cannon stove gave off some warmth at first, but cold crept in the moment it ceased to glow, making our breath turn to steam and causing ice to form on the metal floor under the stove where the water bucket had slopped over as the train rattled on through the night.

After several stops and starts during the night we eventually arrived in Friedland, a small town in the Sudetenland, beyond the Silesian/Czech border – as the crow flies, only about thirty kilometres from Lauban. We wondered what was happening there since we could hear the rumble of war in the distance.

Mother, who had never liked to be in confined spaces, became increasingly more uncomfortable in the blacked-out, over-crowded space that contained us. She then had what we later knew to be her first asthma attack. She had always been a healthy and resolute person who rarely showed weaknesses, but at that point the uncertainty of our situation, and the nagging fear for Father and our home must have hit a vulnerable spot and caused the attack. It frightened her and all who witnessed it. More of these attacks occurred at later dates at stressful times, and eventually contributed to heart problems and her death at the comparatively early age of sixty-one.

Friedland provided a breathing space for us all. The officials in charge of the train were informed that it should remain there for the time being, in case repair facilities were needed if the Russian offensive was halted.

The train was shunted into a siding, and local railway families offered us temporary accommodation. There was the option of travelling on further independently for those who had relatives or another destination to go to. This did not apply to us. So we stayed on, hoping to be able to return home again soon.

Frau Werner, who lived in a railway-owned house near the station, was kind enough to take us in, and was pleased to have some company. Her husband and sons were in the army.

For the next week we existed in a kind of limbo, not knowing what fate had in store for us. Friedland actually lived up to its name – 'peace land'. It was a pretty little town with a castle on the hill and life proceeding calmly and in an orderly fashion. Shops, cinemas, pubs and cafes were open. No one stopped us from exploring the environment a little, seeing films, or having *Ersatzkaffee* and cakes in town. In the evening, Frau Werner made herbal tea while we played board games to while the time away. But the radio news reminded us that war raged in our home region. There was one incident that filled us with foreboding. On one of our daily sorties to the repair unit, still our 'headquarters' at the time, we saw another train standing in the sidings not too far away. It had five or six goods wagons with doors barred with wire mesh. Inside men stood crammed together, clad in grey outfits and tattered blankets, all ashen-faced and hollow-eyed. They were silent and stared into space, seemingly too inert to take an interest in their environment. Who were they? Why were they in that state? Where did they come from? Where were they going? Nobody had an answer to these questions.

We shuddered and turned away, not knowing what to do and what to think other than that there was something spine chillingly sinister about this train.

Much later we heard about the atrocities perpetrated in concentration camps like Auschwitz against Jews and other minority groups. Later still, I read a personal account of a Jew now living in America, who had been transported from Auschwitz to another 'labour camp' near Weimar, where he was liberated by American troops. He recalled a chilly morning on this journey when the wagons were left in a siding for hours till another engine could be found to continue the train journey. It seems that Friedland was on this route. I might have seen him in passing. The vision of this train still haunts me.

For us, hope rose in early March when the news came that the Russians had been beaten back and that Kerzdorf and Lauban were free again. Free, but severely damaged. However, the railway line, the only remaining link between the still unoccupied part of Silesia and the rest of Germany, which had been the object of fierce defence, remained substantially intact. A few days later the rail maintenance unit moved back across the Czech border to be ready for essential repair work.

We stayed with friends in Landeshut, since civilians were still not permitted to enter what was currently considered to be a war zone. There were plenty of rumours, but no one knew for sure what the situation at home was.

The tension was almost unbearable. In the end, some of us threw caution to the wind and embarked on a reconnaissance expedition. In the absence of any public transport facilities, a railway neighbour had the idea of requisitioning a *draisine*, a type of trolley used for inspecting rail tracks. It was a sort of platform on four wheels that could be moved along on the tracks through rocking a lever to and fro to turn the wheels. I suppose it was madness to contemplate such an undertaking, but in the end four of us, including two 'experts', set off in the direction of home on this unconventional vehicle, not knowing how long it would take us to get there. We took turns to keep the wheels moving on hills and slopes, and the rather easier straight runs. After hours of hard labour we rested in a barn. At break of dawn we set off again with aching arms and shoulders, and eventually reached the perimeter of our village.

We had been warned that there was still occasional artillery fire from the Russian line, just a few kilometres away and that we must not use the rail bridge over the River Queis for fear of setting off undetonated charges. So we left our conveyance before the bridge, hidden by vegetation, and scrambled down the embankment on the 'safe' side, heading for the village.

I still remember the chill and desolate feeling of this dull March morning, when we realised that the rumours, which had been circulating, were true. There was an eerie silence, no sign of life. Even the birds had stopped chirping. Acrid smells of smoke and burning hung over the ruins of half the village. Herr

Winkler's house was a smouldering heap of rubble. We all cried, but he just said that he was glad that his wife had taken the children to Munich a few weeks earlier as a precautionary measure.

It looked as if fighting had ceased halfway through the village. The houses in the upper part of it were still standing, albeit with shattered windows, damaged roofs and holes and dents in the walls from artillery fire. The place was deserted.

'Well, we have seen what we came to see,' Herr Winkler said with remarkable composure. 'We have to get back on to the track before it gets dark. Our folks will wonder what has happened to us.'

The *draisine* was still in the place where we left it, but we found it hard going to move it, since the return journey was mainly uphill. We had to abandon it halfway to Landeshut and were lucky to come across a military truck with a sympathetic driver, who gave us a lift to our destination. A week later the whole train and its occupants moved homeward.

Homecoming: Picking up the Pieces

Lauban and adjoining Kerzdorf were one of the last places where, in March 1945, a concentrated effort had been made by the depleted German army to throw back the Russian invaders. They left the town in a smouldering heap of rubble, the streets strewn with disintegrated brickwork, discarded armour, even a disabled tank or two with the dead crews still inside.

'Why do these people have no heads?' my eight-year-old brother asked, when we tried to go to the street where our grandmother had lived, to see if there was any sign of life.

Then I saw the three Russians, propped up against a fence, caked blood on their winter coats, guns still in their hands – their bodies without heads. I was sick and, feeling numb and utterly helpless, we abandoned our excursion and went home again.

After our aborted attempt to go west like many of the villagers, to evade the Russian onslaught, we had returned home when we heard that no further fighting was expected in our area, because the Russian advance was directed towards Berlin.

We were glad to be reunited with Father, who stayed behind with his *Volkssturm* unit. It was only about four weeks since we had left home. Our trolley expedition from Landeshut had shown that the house was still there, if somewhat damaged. What a strange eerie place it had become. It was deadly silent when we entered through the open splintered back door: no clocks ticking or shop bells ringing, or the comforting sound of customers gossiping. It felt as if the building was dead.

Our steps on the flagged floor echoed in the empty space. Occasionally a door banged in the breeze, and blackout blinds flopped in the chilly air streaming through the broken windows. Father checked all the rooms in the house with a stick in his hand, in case he found unwanted intruders, while Mother, Karlheinz and I waited, numb and frightened, in the semi-dark hallway, barely daring to breathe in the stale air.

There was a big gap in the sitting room where the piano and the radio with its octagonal loudspeaker had been. Who would want to steal a piano while war was raging outside? It took some time to find out what else had been taken, what had been destroyed or what was still usable.

Mother cried when she saw the slashed feather beds, soiled with human excrement and the contents of smashed preserving jars. Father looked grim, but heaved a sigh of relief when he realised that his prized baking oven and most of the baking implements appeared to be undamaged in the bakehouse.

There was no electricity to light lamps or the single electric heater we had. No water came out of the taps.

Since there was nowhere else to go, we realised we just had to cope with this trying situation. We were cold, thirsty, hungry and very weary. Mother was the first to regain composure and decided with her usual common sense and determination: 'We'd better try to sort some of this mess out before it gets dark. We need food, drink and somewhere to sleep.'

The old pump in the yard was still working – so a water supply was assured. The fuel sheds in the yard had been broken open, but still contained a good stock of wood and anthracite to light the kitchen stove and make Father hopeful that he would be able to get his baking oven going again eventually.

We found some matches and a supply of candles in the Christmas decoration box. Father also managed to light the carbide lamp from his old bicycle, which hissed and spluttered before it lit up properly, but was very bright. However, it gave off peculiar fumes and could not be used inside. The oil lamp from Grandmother's flat was better for this purpose.

We found some unsoiled bedding in her flat too, and decided to use her bedroom for all of us to sleep in since the single window there was still intact.

The cellar smelt musty from lack of airing but contained enough basic food to keep us going for a while: a heap of potatoes which had been stored for the winter, crocks half full of sauerkraut and gherkins. Several bottles of home-made beer still stood in the recess in the wall where we had put them to mature. There was also a large chunk of yeast, dried up on the outside but still usable in the centre. Later, it provided the starting ingredient for new bread baking. Among the debris of smashed preserving jars, one or two glasses of berries and liver pâté were intact. So were a few pieces of speck – smoked fat bacon – hanging from the ceiling, and strings of dried apple slices, which provided ready-made comfort food.

Once the kitchen stove was lit we were able to have some lime-blossom tea. The herbal tea box had not been raided. We found some rusks in the shop, also some stale bread, which Mother converted into 'poor man's soup', along with some margarine from the bakery and some still usable garlic cloves. Father had on occasions made this dish for himself, even when more sophisticated foods were available. It was just a matter of laying slices of stale bread into a soup bowl, slicing garlic over this, adding a little salt and a knob of butter and pouring boiling water over it. It tasted wonderful that day and we felt better for it.

Later we warmed a couple of bricks on the hot stove, wrapped them in old newspapers and used them to warm the beds in Grandmother's chilly room. We slept quite well after that, being exhausted.

The next day we cautiously explored the neighbourhood and found a few villagers who had returned to their homes or who had miraculously survived the fighting and pillaging in their cellars and outhouses. Old Herr Maier had hidden in a hut on his allotment, and survived by eating winter cabbages and stored carrots when his emergency rations had run out.

Our aunt's flat next door was empty but we heard that a farmer friend had taken both her and Grandmother, who was unable to walk, by cart to his farm in Steinkirch, a village a few miles away and just outside the war zone. The whereabouts of other family members remained unclear.

We had no means of communicating with the outside world: no telephone, mail, newspapers or electricity to switch on a surviving radio.

Then a truck with military personnel arrived, reminding us that war was still in progress. It was a supply unit, looking for a place to park their vehicles, to take stock and find further sources of food supplies.

When they heard that there was a baker with a usable bake-house in the otherwise devastated area, they enlisted Father's help to replenish their stores. He was only too glad to oblige. He had some flour left in the attic store and the soldiers supplied more and offered help on the production line. The baking had to be done at night since a smoking chimney might attract enemy attention in daylight.

We now had some contact with the wider world again and heard that the Russians were rapidly advancing towards Berlin, but we were still considered to be in the official war zone, where only essential personnel was supposed to be present. Mother, as bakery helper, fell into that category, but my brother and I were urged to move to a safer place. Forays to find relatives in Lauban, as we had attempted to do, were definitely frowned upon, since we might encounter not only dead Russians but landmines or undetonated ammunition on our hike to town.

We did not really want to leave home again but had to obey orders, so mounted our bikes and cycled to Steinkirch to join my aunt and grandmother at Dietrich's farm.

We were able to take some bread and cake along. The soldiers had given Mother the ingredients for the crumble cake as a treat for the family. We heard that once the bread was in the oven in the late evenings they joined my parents in the sitting room and produced proper coffee beans and liqueurs to celebrate the survival of another day, while listening to Radio Belgrade and Lale Anderson singing 'Lily Marlene'.

The unit was suddenly called away a week or so later. Father continued to bake bread once or twice a week, having located a source of more flour. In order to get it he had to push a wheel-barrow over a makeshift bridge to the mill on the other side of the River Queis – quite a dangerous undertaking. Still, it kept him happy. He needed to be useful and obviously provided a necessary service for the villagers who were still there. Nobody objected when my brother and I came home again.

Resuming daily routines lulled us into a false sense of security. We even ventured out again to pick catkins and meadow anem-ones as well as *huflattich* blossoms for Mother's tea chest. They flower in early April. However, by the end of the month we were on the move again, trying to get away from a new wave of Russian invaders.

This time the farmer, who had given Tante Grete, my grandmother, my brother and me temporary shelter, offered to put some of our belongings on his horse-drawn cart. We walked behind the wagon, and slowly edged our way towards the Czech border, along with withdrawing military personnel – the dregs of what was left of the once proud German army, unable or possibly unwilling to offer any more resistance.

We had heard that Hitler was dead, and that the German troops on the Western Front had capitulated to the Allies, the American and British forces, but that the Russians were still at war to complete their conquest of Berlin, and presumably gain as much German territory as possible.

A sense of panic and hysteria pervaded the early days of May 1945 for those of us exposed to the onslaught of the Red Army. We felt trapped.

All we thought of was trying to put as many miles as possible between us and the raiding, robbing and raping hordes from the East, although realistically there was little hope of reaching the River Elbe and the lands beyond that were now occupied by the Allies and promised a less traumatic existence.

On 9 May 1945 the war on the Eastern Front ended as well. We sat on a hillside in Christophsgrund, a hamlet just beyond the Czech border, exhausted and thirsty after miles of trekking along rutted roads in the burning afternoon sun.

With disbelief and horror we saw a row of tanks approaching the village, dusty and dirt-encrusted and unmistakably Russian. Mother had another severe asthma attack.

The Russian Experience

The spearhead of tanks did not stop, but soon other armoured vehicles followed, as we scrambled off the embankment and tried to seek refuge in the nearby farmhouses. The convoy stopped, and fierce-looking soldiers not only demanded water to drink, but relieved terrified villagers of watches, rings, coins, pocket knives, even the odd thermos flask. With glee they snatched up packets of cigarettes and bottles of beer, which had fallen off the back of a lorry when it toppled into a bomb crater caused by a stray Russian plane.

The inhabitants of the hamlet readily offered us shelter in their homes, outbuildings, stables and haystacks. Four of us crept into the straw of an empty cubicle in the pigsty. Out of sight of the marauding soldiers, over the squeaking and grunting of the pigs we could hear the shouting and screams of women being raped in the farmyard.

Tante Grete and I experienced our share of violence on the next day when we tried to dig up some potatoes from a winter store behind the farm. A group of raiders appeared from nowhere and started shooting, not to kill us, but to stop us from running away. I have never before felt as terrified as I did then. Being raped by brutish, smelly strangers is definitely not an ideal way to lose one's virginity, but at least no permanent damage was done and I survived to tell the tale. Mental scars eventually faded, but a scar above my left ankle, caused by a piece of shrapnel, remains a reminder of this ordeal.

There was no time for self-pity in those days. Again, decisions had to be made about our future. We could not live in a pigsty in Christophsgrund forever, kind as our hosts were.

Farmer Dietrich's horses and wagon had been requisitioned, so we loaded what belongings we still had, together with our surprisingly uncomplaining grandmother, on to our *leiterwagen*, a hand-drawn cart with ladder-like sides, for the trek back home where we hoped to find Father. We avoided main roads as far as possible, and actually encountered little harassment on our weary walk back to Kerzdorf.

Father was just as glad to see us as we were to find him in our house where he had been since his *Volkssturm* unit had been disbanded on ceasefire day, about ten days earlier.

After the gruelling days in Christophsgrund, home felt like heaven. It was good to be in familiar surroundings again, to have a roof over our head, leaky as it was, and to sleep in a bed without fear of bombing and shelling, now that war was over. There was also no need to scrounge or beg for food now.

Still, it was a very uneasy peace that prevailed. There was no guarantee of personal safety. Almost daily, Russians entered the house uninvited to confiscate items that might be of use to them: pots, pans, our little spirit stove, tools and bicycles from the shed. Objects of any value, like our faithful old radio, the piano, and the wall clocks had long since gone. The only timepiece we had left was an old wind-up alarm clock. We almost laughed when we saw one of the Russian officers ride around on Mother's bike clad in Father's flannelette pyjamas, probably thinking they were acceptable summer wear on a warm, late-May day. Someone else collected his food ration from the communal kitchen using Grandmother's chamber pot.

Fearful of further assaults, I stayed in my small bedroom with a wardrobe hiding the door. Father had loosened a back panel of this piece of furniture, which could be slid aside for me to enter and leave my hiding place.

I am still not sure why one of the villagers 'denounced' me, so to speak. I had to abandon my safe haven to join the forced labour contingent. Every day a group of Russians stalked through the village, shouting: '*Rabotta – daway, daway!*' rounding up as many able–bodied men and women as they could find to do whatever work they had in mind for them. Mother and Father were allowed to stay at home to get the bakery into working order again, since the troops could not rely on their own provisions.

Around fifty of us were marched away, wondering what 'Rabotta' was in store for us. We had heard that some people had been forced to walk slowly, arms linked, over a minefield, to clear the area. I can imagine the terror they must have felt with every step they took. As it happened, there were no mines, so luckily no one came to harm.

The men in my group were given shovels and buckets to clear the roads of rubble and other debris left from the fighting days. More than once they found smelly, decaying body parts of victims, too far gone to be identified.

With a dozen or so other women I was marched off to the smartest part of Lauban, where some of the palatial villas of local industrialists had survived the war in a reasonable state. We were made to clean the places, scrub the floors, move furniture about and so on, ready for the occupation by the new administrators.

We had no idea who they might be. At the time, we were totally isolated from the wider world. There were no newspapers, radios or telephones to keep us informed of what was going on elsewhere, or what was going to happen to us. We lived in hope that one of these days the Russians would depart, which would allow us to pick up the pieces and to re-establish some sort of normality.

We could not believe it at first when rumours spread that there had been a conference by the victors of the war, where decisions were made to separate Silesia from Germany to become a Polish province. Still, we soon realised that there must be some truth in this when a young Pole established himself in the former *Bürgermeister's* office and began to issue orders. All Germans had to be registered, and were told to wear white armbands with a blue stripe to distinguish them from Polish or Russian residents.

Russian army personnel were gradually withdrawing from the area, but not before they had dismantled such industrial fixtures as might be of use to them. The contents of the *Unterwerk*, the centre from where the electric train lines in the region had been operated, seemed to be of particular interest to them. Men worked day and night to take out the intricate machines, transformers and switchgear panels, and to load them on to trains to be transported to Russia for reassembly in some part of Siberia. The former chief engineer of the *Unterwerk* was ordered to accompany the dismantled equipment, but managed to abscond before the train set off, knowing that the complicated apparatus could never be correctly reassembled, since it had been taken out in a haphazard way. No one had thought to label items, and they had damaged essential components. Some bulky pieces were lowered to ground level through holes in the wall and crash-landed.

My Russian registration, May 1945

A Polish Work Certificate, February 1946

New Masters

Early in June a train full of Polish families arrived in Lauban and began to take possession of any properties they fancied. Many dwellings were empty anyway, since the owners had managed to flee the Russian onslaught and had not returned to the village.

Strangers came to inspect our premises, and then one Pole indicated that he was the new owner of the house and bakery, but that he would permit us to stay and work there as before. There was nothing we could do about this – no one to complain to, since this 'resettlement' happened with the full approval of our Russian and Polish masters.

New rumours circulated in mid-June. We heard that in Middle and Upper Silesia all remaining Germans had been evicted from their homes. Cattle trains full of displaced people had apparently been seen crossing the Oder/Neisse line, which was said to be the new border between Silesia and German territory. We lived in fear that we might be evicted as well.

We were. Without prior warning. Militiamen banged on every door where Germans were still living, telling us to assemble in the middle of the village, carrying just hand luggage. No trains or other means of transport awaited us. So on Sunday 24 June 1945, six weeks after the war was over, stern-looking armed militiamen made us walk and eventually drag ourselves over twenty kilometres to the newly established Polish/German border, through woodland and fields, bypassing any villages on the way. Once we had crossed a footbridge over the Neisse, our guards dumped us in a meadow and left us to fend for ourselves.

I can't remember much about that first night after our expulsion. We dropped down with exhaustion. It was cold and dark, and the grass was wet. The only one who was not hungry was our little pet goat, whom my eight-year-old brother had insisted on bringing along tethered in a dog collar. She found plenty of grass and herbs to munch and then shared our uncomfortable night quarters.

When the sun rose next morning we found that a group of local people was staring at us bemusedly: after all, we were a bedraggled heap of strangers who seemed to have appeared from nowhere. They could barely believe what we told them, then rallied round to bring some food and drink, and offer at least some of us temporary accommodation.

Some folks set off to find friends or relatives who lived in the Görlitz area where we found ourselves. We – Mother, Father, my two brothers, two aunts and, of course, Grandmother and the little goat – decided to try to reach Niesky, where we hoped to find some distant relatives. This meant another couple of days walk, but by now we were almost used to this perpetual roaming.

Werner, the elder of my two brothers, was then with us again. Although only sixteen he had been recruited to an army support group in February 1945. He was captured and released by Allied Forces in Germany when the war ended, and had walked the hundreds of kilometres to return home to Kerzdorf in late May of that year.

Niesky

Our stay at Niesky proved to be just another episode in our stop-start existence. We found our relatives' – the Springers' – house unoccupied. There were no neighbours to tell us where they had gone, and we had yet to find any local officials who could help or advise us. Not knowing where else we could turn, we moved in without explicit permission. The door was open and the place had been ransacked, but we managed to restore some sort of order. Anything was better than sleeping in a damp meadow, or in stables and haylofts, which tended to cause Mother severe breathing problems. At one stage we feared she might choke to death – a frightening experience for all of us. On the latest trek, our little goat had injured her leg on barbed wire and had to be left behind on a farm, where the farmer's young daughter promised to look after her.

Our new abode was a quite modern house, with taps in the kitchen, a bathroom and a flushing toilet, but none of these worked. We devised our own primitive way of sewage disposal in the back garden and found a working pump in a yard nearby. It was July, and warm, so heating was not a problem. There was enough spare wood lying about in the area to light the kitchen stove to boil water for safety's sake, and to start cooking the moment we had something to cook.

We found some old potatoes in the cellar, happily sprouting, but still edible. The garden yielded some berries and herbs, notably peppermint, which became a staple in our diet. We discovered a bank of chanterelles in a copse nearby – a pity we had no butter to fry them in.

A few days later, Father came back from one of his exploratory trips, somewhat unsteady on his legs but triumphant, clutching a piece of bread and a slice of speck in his hands. He had combed the area, accompanied by Karlheinz, looking out for local tradesmen who might have something to sell or who might even offer some opportunity to work.

They came across a group of Russians who were trying to make sense of the workings of a modern baking oven in an outhouse behind a closed bakery. Father daringly offered his assistance. He knew a few Russian and Polish phrases by now, and gestures helped to make the strangers understand that he was just the person they needed to solve their problems. They seemed very pleased and urged him to start '*rabotta*' the next morning. They shook hands with him and Karlheinz, and offered vodka to seal the deal. They invariably carried bottles of vile spirits and pieces of speck in their pockets.

Father just hoped that he would have no serious difficulties in getting the baking oven to operate again. Thankfully, all went well. The next day the Russians brought coal and the required ingredients for him to get on with the job. So for the next few weeks Father became the official baker for the engineering corps, which was responsible for dismantling any usable plant and machinery in the area so that it could eventually be transported to Russia. No money changed hands, but the provisions he was given improved our standard of living considerably.

Father was in his element, feeling useful again, but the rest of us were somewhat wary of this arrangement and watched with trepidation when two young Russians walked up the garden path and rapped on the window. They had actually not come to steal things or assault us, but to bring gifts – some sugar, flour, semolina and more speck. '*Kuh kaput, kuh kaput,*' one of them shouted, indicating that he wanted us to give him a bowl or other receptacle. A little later he returned with meat from a cow that had just been slaughtered. He beamed, obviously pleased with himself, and then spent some time kicking a ball around the garden with Karlheinz.

An officer who came to inspect Father's unusual working arrangements could speak German, and praised his skill. He wanted to know what Father was doing in Niesky when he had his own bakery elsewhere. He knew for sure that Silesia, beyond the local river, the Neisse, had been ceded to Poland but was unaware of the implications of this for the native German population. He was quite sympathetic to our plight and made it known that he and his fellow soldiers did not trust the Poles at all.

Mutual antagonism often caused difficulties when Russian trains wanted to cross the border. He also indicated that his unit's tasks were almost completed, and in the end they would dismantle the fancy baking oven as well, to take home with them on the train, which would be full of other spoils of war.

In the meantime rumour had it that the Poles in Lauban and Kerzdorf realised that they had been rather rash in evicting what was left of the native population, since no one else was left to maintain essential local services. In fact, we were told that they would not mind if villagers returned home of their own accord. It was Herr Reissaus who brought this news. As the village daredevil he had survived a spell in a concentration camp during Hitler's time for offences against the state – in his case, for listening to foreign broadcasts, and for black marketing activities. He now made regular reconnaissance trips across the Neisse to our home area to find out what was going on there. He knew where and when it was best to do these illegal excursions, swimming or wading through shallow parts of the river, and he also knew where one might find a usable boat.

As a consequence, Father decided to go back to Kerzdorf once his services were dispensed with and the Russians prepared to leave the area. The Polish *Starosta*, the village administrator, had no objections when Father reoccupied his own house. Other villagers had returned too and began to re-establish services, like the local water supply and disposal.

A week later, Herr Reissaus accompanied Mother and my brothers personally over the border to join Father. Tante Hanne's business and house no longer existed, so she decided to go west to find some friends who lived in the Rheinland. This left Tante Grete and me in Niesky to look after Grandmother, who was definitely not fit to swim, wade or row a little boat across the Neisse. We hoped that legal border travel would be allowed soon. After all, over three months had passed since the war had ended.

Home Again… and Away

August 1945

One evening Ivan, the German-speaking Russian, came to see us. He knew that Father had repatriated himself, and offered us help with travel into Silesia if we wanted to go home. His engineering corps was leaving Niesky, with Russia as the ultimate destination, but Lauban was en route and not too far away. We could have a free ride there. He promised to make sure that the *babushka*, the old lady, would be made comfortable, and we would be well hidden in one of the goods wagons, to escape Polish controls at the river bridge. He would also make sure that the train halted near Lauban under some pretext to allow us to get out and away.

Grandmother's yearning to go home and our precarious situation persuaded us to accept this unusual offer. It was only later when we reached familiar territory and clambered down the embankment on the last lap of our trip that we fully realised all the things that could have gone wrong. We could have been apprehended for trespassing on military territory while hanging about by the siding. Since there was no definite departure time given for the train, we had to be at the goods yard in the morning. We only had Ivan's word to say that it was all right for us to be there. We felt utterly out of place and exposed. Noting some activity in the field kitchen area, I offered help, in order not to feel absolutely useless. We must have looked a strange tableau, sitting on railway sleepers, peeling potatoes, with an old woman looking on, her legs dangling from the handcart in which she sat and asking why 'those people', who continued to load machinery on to the train, talked in a funny language. The meal of potato, bean and pork hotpot offered to us by the portly cook in the afternoon was very good.

Eventually, instead of heaving another tractor on to the train, strong arms picked Grandmother and her handcart up, and found a place for her and us in one of the loaded wagons. When the train left around ten that evening we travelled in a sealed wagon laden with loosely tethered agricultural machinery, which moved precariously when the engine steamed off. It would have been difficult to get out at this stage if we had wanted to get away. There was a lot of shouting and swearing in Russian and Polish at the border and shots were fired. Some shunting took place and some wagons were detached from the train for some reason. Luckily, our wagon remained attached to the engine. We might have ended up in a siding, unable get out or attract attention. What if Ivan had been unable to stop the train near home as he had promised? We could have ended up in Siberia. As it happened, Ivan was able to keep his word and deposited our handcart and us more or less in the same spot where we had left the *draisine* a few months ago on our reconnaissance mission from Landeshut.

We were glad to be reunited with the rest of the family but could not help wondering what was going to happen next, hoping that prevailing circumstances were transitory and life would eventually go back to normal. We had yet to see any official evidence of the fate of Silesia. Rumour continued to be the only form of news.

Only a fraction of the original village population of about 1,700 had returned to the area, and the sounds we heard around us were overwhelmingly Polish. More families from Eastern Poland came and occupied empty houses or requisitioned others they took a fancy to. However, only a few settled down when they realised that their new territory was not paved with gold and already stripped of most desirable objects.

Hard work and determination were required to make a reasonable living in an area where most economic foundations no longer existed. Former employment opportunities in the cotton and linen industry and in the railway engineering works had gone. Lauban itself, and part of Kerzdorf, were in ruins and unrepaired dwellings were exposed to all weathers.

Untended gardens and fields turned to wasteland. There were few shops since there was nothing to sell other than the most basic commodities – bread when flour was available to bake it, some garden and farm produce if anyone had a little surplus to sell, and milk which had often turned sour before it reached the customers. Still, the Poles seemed to like sour milk and drank it about as avidly as their vodka. This was also rarely available to buy either, so they began to distil their own spirits from grain and potatoes.

Father and Herr Reissaus tried their hands at it too. The whole house reeked of fermenting potato mash for days and the resulting liquor was very potent but tasted vile, mainly of burnt sugar beet, which had been added to the other ingredients so that the sugar content might enhance conversion to alcohol. This was the only attempt at vodka production they made.

We were lucky to have something to barter with – a loaf of bread for fresh milk or some eggs and occasionally meat or a boiling fowl from a farmer who had still some livestock left. So, once again, Father's trade proved to be an advantage for us.

One day Lena, a rather forceful, haughty, Polish woman officer moved into a house near us. We had no idea what type of position she held, but soon realised that she was feared and deferred to. She was known to strike out with a horsewhip if people did not do her bidding.

I was ordered to do her cleaning and the laundry. When she came to inspect our premises she appointed Father as her personal baker. Although resources were generally very limited she managed to procure ingredients for cakes and other confectionery for her parties and official guests. She brought mouth-watering joints of beef or pork to be roasted in the baking oven. At Christmas, the scent of roasting geese permeated the house. When basting the birds, Mother ladled a little goose fat and juices into a bowl; this was later used for the flavouring of the red cabbage we ate with our Christmas roast chicken. Our bartering resources did not stretch to geese or ducks, but we felt rich compared with the deprivation we had experienced earlier in the year.

Lena had heard that Mother was quite good at sewing, so when her live-in friend Maria decided to get married to one of the militia officers, she made her minions find a sewing machine, which actually looked very much like the one which had been stolen from us. Looted material was thus converted into quite passable party dresses by Pani Elsa, my Mother. Her hairdressing skills were also put to the test. She still had some ancient curling tongs that, in skilled hands and when heated over a spirit flame, could produce waves and shingled hair. Lena and Maria walked down the village in their new silk dresses, and were barely recognisable with their fancy hairstyles.

Father was roped in to play the piano at the wedding banquet, but luckily escaped before the party became too rowdy. A lot of vodka was consumed, and a cigarette ignited the settee. Lena ended up with singed hair and wore a turban for a while. She had apparently tried to douse the flames with vodka before someone poured a bucket of water over both her and the settee.

Not long after this, Lena and her coterie suddenly left the area. She did not tell us that she was going, and strangely enough we missed this colourful character.

Since we still lived our days in ignorance of the political situation, we had tried to find out through her what was going on, but she had had no answers for us. Inquiries at the *Starosta* office met with equally vague responses. It seemed that as long as we worked and were useful, we had nothing to fear. Still, it became increasingly clear that we had to accept that Silesia had ceased to be the German province, which it had been for hundreds of years.

There had been several 'landlords' who claimed to own our premises, but neither Oleg, Yurek nor Tadek were around for long. They all wanted their share of profit from the shop once money (in the form of zloties) was in circulation again, but they found it too tiresome to look for and buy the raw materials we needed to bake and trade. Oleg was cheeky enough to ask Father to buy the bakery from him.

When another new owner, Marek, arrived in January 1946, we were told that while working arrangements would continue as before, we had to move out since he needed the living quarters for nine family members and 'jedne crowa' – a cow.

Once again, we packed our few belongings and found accommodation with some innkeeper friends just a few doors away from our house. We regretted now that we had ever come back from Niesky, but, as Grandmother said, where should we have gone from there? Returning to the family home seemed to be the only option at the time.

We were, of course, not the only ones to find ourselves in this dilemma. Other villagers who had returned home after the June eviction were in the same boat. Although official meetings of Germans were forbidden, we came together occasionally to discuss our situation, let off steam, and indulge in hopeful thinking that one day we might wake up to find that the last year had just been a bad dream. In the meantime, we just lived one day at a time as best as we could.

When spring came, Herr Reissaus resumed his fact-finding trips and brought news from Kohlfurt, the border town through which we passed on Ivan's goods train. He told us that once again trains full of expelled Germans were passing through, but that now an international organisation directed operations. He thought it would not be too difficult for anyone who wanted to get away to take this route westward into Germany. One or two villagers took advantage of this.

I toyed with this idea too, since life for me was becoming more and more intolerable. I did not mind working and even put up with customers swearing when I had to tell them yet again that there was *niema chleba* or *niema buki*, no more bread or rolls, since supplies usually ran out well before the shop closed, but I resented being leered at and pawed by male customers who thought they did me a favour by being 'nice' to me. One was particularly persistent and wanted me to move in with him as his housekeeper, a prospect that made me almost physically sick.

A former schoolmate found herself in a similar position. We began to give serious thought to absconding, for sheer self-preservation.

Once our parents realised that life for us was not only frustrating but almost intolerable, they reluctantly gave their blessings if we wanted to leave. Herr Reissaus kept us informed of events in Kohlfurt, and offered his services as a guide there.

In mid-April I packed my few belongings into a rucksack and said a tearful goodbye to my family and the home village. Gerda, my friend, backed out of the arrangement at the last moment and I hesitated briefly about carrying on by myself, but after all the soul-searching of the last few weeks and the traumatic farewell, I resolved not to turn back, but to make the fateful journey into an unknown future.

It was still dark outside when I met Herr Reissaus near the railway goods yard, where we were able to hitch a lift on an empty coal train. We still had a few miles to go when the train stopped at its own destination. Luckily, my companion knew the area like the back of his hand, and could warn me of obstacles like barbed wire barriers as we scrambled through the heath and woodland towards Kohlfurt.

It must have been around eight in the morning when we reached the perimeter of the station. There was no time to lose. I was near to having a panic attack when my guide, having accomplished his mission, vanished down the embankment, leaving me to my own devices.

The nearest rail-tracks obviously had not been used for ages and were overgrown with brushwood and littered with coal and other debris. I carefully wound my way around a couple of empty, stationary goods trains and then found the platform teeming with people of all ages carrying bags and bundles of their possessions. The almost silent, subdued crowd took no notice of me as I tried to find the shortest queue in front of one of the desks manned by uniformed officials, who registered the collection of people who no longer had a home to go to. They issued permits for one of the trains, which were to take us westward over the border.

The whole operation was run by UNRRA, the United Nations Relief and Rehabilitation Administration, staffed by English-speaking men and woman and some Red Cross helpers.

The contents of my rucksack and shoulder bag were inspected and the papers I had were looked at with interest. Then I was sprayed with some white powder from top to bottom to kill any vermin I might carry. I found out later that the stuff was called DDT. I had never heard of this before.

Another thing that was new to me was the range of drinks and sandwiches we were offered. I certainly was thirsty and liked the milky tea and the fluffy white bread with jam to go with it. I knew then what Sergeant Douglas meant when he said that his fellow prisoners just could not chew the firm rye bread, which was our staple diet at home.

Sergeant Douglas had been the liaison officer of a group of British prisoners of war who lived in an encampment near the village and worked in the local quarry. He had become quite friendly with Father, and took an interest in our family and village life in general. Officially, this fraternisation was definitely frowned upon, but one could not help liking this polite, smart Englishman who could easily have outpaced his somewhat lame *Volkssturm* prison guards when he came to collect the prisoners' bread rations. Father had seen no reason why he should not give them white bread instead of the coarse rye bread they were supposed to be issued with. The prisoners left well before the Russians reached the area. They did not relish being 'liberated' by their allies.

Among the few papers I treasured and carried with me on my last day in Silesia was one with Mr Douglas' address in England. He had given it to us as a possible contact point if war events should make us lose contact with other family members. His predictions of an 'uneasy peace' had unfortunately come true.

By mid-afternoon, we were allocated a space on the straw-covered floor of a goods wagon, ready for the trip over the border. Most of my fellow travellers had been expelled from their homes in Middle Silesia. Nobody felt like talking.

Eventually we crossed the bridge over the Neisse. Eight months before we had travelled on the same route on Ivan's train, but in the opposite direction. We had different hopes and aspirations then – certainly we had not expected to lose our homes and rights as German citizens in Silesia.

I felt very sad and tearful that evening and overwhelmingly alone, but drifted off to sleep from sheer exhaustion while the train rattled and clanked westward through the middle of Germany, which by then had become the Russian Zone. We had reached the English Zone when the morning chill and daylight woke me.

The reception camp was somewhere near Obisfelde, later a crossing point for travellers beyond the Iron Curtain. We were greeted with porridge, more fluffy bread and tea, while some registration formalities proceeded. By late evening we continued our journey, this time in a proper and quite comfortable passenger train. We passed Braunschweig and Hanover and then lesser-known towns like Cloppenburg and Heidemuhle till the journey came to an end in Jever in Friesland, not far from the North Sea's coast. About twenty of us were loaded on to a lorry and taken to Sengwarden, a small village seemingly in the middle of nowhere.

Whatever the future held, I did not regret having left the perpetual harassment and humiliation behind me, and was hopeful now that I would be able to gain a measure of control over my life again.

Sengwarden

Herr Vienup stood at the edge of the small village green and, like the other villagers there, must have viewed the strangers who were deposited from the back of a lorry with suspicion and apprehension.

This was the first time that the inhabitants of Sengwarden had been asked to accommodate a consignment of 'expellees' or displaced persons. The more central areas of West Germany were already saturated with homeless people. Some of them lost their homes in bombing raids. Others had fled the Eastern provinces to escape the Russian onslaught, and were now unable to return to their homes. On top of all this, new waves of homeless people arrived who had been expelled when formerly Eastern provinces of Germany, like Silesia, were handed over to the Poles.

Herr Vienup was a sturdy, elderly man, wearing a blue and white striped butcher's apron. He reminded me of my father, who had often gone out into the village or even to Lauban proudly wearing a white starched apron as a sign of his trade. Herr Vienup saw me standing alone with my bundle of possessions and offered to take me home to his family.

I don't remember details of my first encounter with them, but can only say that I was made very welcome. They probably felt pity for the *lutte dern* (little girl, in Plattdeutsch language), who had nowhere to go on Easter Saturday.

It was strange to be transported in to an environment that seemed to have been untouched by war and its aftermath.

Easter passed in a haze for me. The Vienups, their daughter, her fiancé and countless visitors asked endless questions about my background and the events that brought me there. I had some difficulties understanding the Plattdeutsche dialect, but tried hard to satisfy their curiosity, though getting wearier by the hour. I remember drinking countless cups of tea, made the Friesian way: a lump of sugar was placed into a small porcelain cup and black tea poured over. This would dissolve part of the sugar but leave more behind when the liquid was drunk. More tea would then be added and the process repeated till the sugar had gone. Thick slices of butter cake with custard filling accompanied this beverage. I could barely cope with the platter of cold meats served for supper later and dropped off to sleep after Herr Vienup insisted that I tried a glass of 'Grog'.

Lisa, Vienup's only daughter, then twenty-three, did not object to my sharing her room. She was getting married in the near future and said I could have the room to myself after that.

After the uncertain and unpredictable existence I had left behind, I could barely believe that people could live such ordered and normal lives and could get worked up about such trivial issues as the colour of the tablecloth for Lisa's wedding meal, and the length of her dress.

Feeling very much out of touch with events in Germany and in the wider world, I avidly read every old and new newspaper and magazine I could get hold of, in order to fill wide gaps in my knowledge. I was the one who asked endless questions now, which people found rather quaint. Was it possible that someone did not know that the war with Japan went on till August of the previous year and only ended when the Americans dropped atom bombs on Japanese cities? War trials were held in Munich and some of the previous Nazi chiefs had committed suicide or were condemned to death or long incarceration.

To be able to listen to the radio again was wonderful. I lapped up not only the news and the commentaries but also the musical offerings.

I also learned that it was conferences held by the Allied leaders in Yalta and Potsdam that decided Germany's fate after the war. There the decisions were made to create military zones within the country and to draw a new eastern border along the Oder/Neisse line. The Oder was the largest river in Silesia, and the Neisse one of its tributaries. The Neisse and part of the Oder made an effective natural dividing line between the Russian occupied zone of Germany and the provinces given to Poland.

I realised that friends and relatives now lived in different zones within Germany under the jurisdiction of different military governors. However, travel and communications within the Western Zones presented few difficulties, while the borders of the Russian Zone were guarded. Other former German parts like Silesia and Westpreussen were now totally out of bounds. It took several weeks after my arrival in Sengwarden before one of my many letters eventually reached my parents, who till then had not known what happened to me once I crossed the Neisse border.

Gradually I managed to re-establish contact with a cousin, who was now living in Bamberg in the American Zone, with former schoolmates in the Rheinland, in the English Zone, and with my uncle in Berlin in the Russian Zone. The village postmistress was quite excited when I received a letter from England. I had informed Sergeant Douglas of our fate and got a very friendly and encouraging letter in return, and heard through him that Werner was now living in Bielefeld. I awaited the postman every day with bated breath and heaved a sigh of relief when I at last got a postcard from my parents in Kerzdorf. They remained there for another year after that, being classed as essential workers. By the time they were eventually evicted no further displaced persons were allowed into the Western Zones, and they had to start a new life near Dresden. It was fortunate that Lisa had once worked in a stationary shop and had a surplus of writing materials, which she kindly shared with me. I seemed to be forever writing letters.

Needless to say, official matters had to be attended to as well. I had to register with the *Bürgermeister* of the area, the *Wohnungsamt* (housing department), apply for food and clothing coupons, and register at the *Arbeitsamt* (the labour exchange) as a job seeker, being very conscious that what little money I had been able to bring along would not last forever. I certainly did not wish to rely on the goodness and generosity of the Vienups for any length of time. Actually, we came to an agreement quite early on: I would earn my keep through working for them. I seemed to have come just at the right time, when *schummeln* (spring cleaning) was in progress, which the locals took very seriously. It was almost as if a competition was on as to who could wear out the most scrubbing brushes. Every cupboard and drawer was emptied completely and thoroughly scrubbed. They were then put into the yard to dry.

The exterior of the house did not escape attention either. It was a good job that the houses were low and squat, which tended to be the case in the area: not only were the windows polished to perfection but the walls were washed as well with long-handled brooms, and the pavements scrubbed.

I learned some more unusual things to do, among them, splicing feathers for Lisa's feather beds. Grandmother and her elderly friends used to do this when I was a little girl and we still kept a gaggle of geese. They sat in the kitchen on winter evenings, ripping the fluffy bits off the middle rib of each feather while gossiping and drinking grain coffee. The air would be thick with floating down, which clung to hair and clothing, but also made wonderfully warm and light duvets and pillows.

Once I went with Herr Vienup, who was retired, and a group of others, into the marshes to cut peat. The men were doing the digging and I helped to stack the brick-shaped blocks for drying – it was back breaking work.

But before I had a chance to get the hang of milking the Vienup's temperamental cow, I was on the move again.

I had been to see a job adviser in Wilhelmshaven and realised that there were no chances of picking up my education and training which had been so rudely interrupted by the end-of-war events. Shop, office and manual jobs could be had, but it was next to impossible to find cheap, suitable accommodation in the overcrowded towns. For me, the only realistic option at the time was to get a live-in position. The Vienups were only too glad to have temporary help in exchange for board and lodging, but I needed to earn some money again and to expand my horizons.

Soon after my visit to Wilhelmshaven, Fräulein Tjaden the job advisor, phoned me, saying that a family she knew were looking for a *Haustochter* – a kind of au pair girl, who would help run the household for a family of six, including two children aged eight and nine, who needed supervision with their homework. The conditions of employment seemed reasonable, and Varel, the place where they lived, quite a congenial little town, not quite as remote as Sengwarden. So, about two months after leaving Kerzdorf, I became a paid employee again.

Varel

I spent the next two years in this small town near Oldenburg, steeped in domesticity.

The Thorbeckes were a well-established local family. They had a wholesale tobacco business that, however, had been near to a standstill since the end of the war, since tobacco goods were virtually unobtainable from importers. So the shelves in the storerooms were empty, although I suspect some little reserves were tucked away somewhere, which could be called upon to provide the odd little luxuries for special occasions.

Opa Thorbecke, now almost redundant, had thrown himself wholeheartedly into horticultural pursuits. He had converted a building site near to the house into a huge garden, which made the household self-sufficient where fruit and vegetables were concerned, Hen pens and rabbit hutches also yielded food supplies.

When Oma Thorbecke was not busy running the household, she dug, planted and harvested too, but the younger couple were less enthusiastic about this. Of course, young Herr Thorbecke still spent some time trying to locate sources of goods for sale, but he also liked to make the rounds of potential customers in pubs and shops once tobacco was available again. He was also quite an accomplished painter, and had a little studio tucked away behind the offices. On Sundays he sometimes cooked the most delicious rabbit stew.

Young Frau Thorbecke evaded work whenever she could. After my arrival even the care of Jochen (nine) and Hilde (eight) fell substantially to me, and food shopping became my responsibility. There were still lots of shortages in 1947 and queuing for bread, meat and dairy products, even sugar, was the rule rather than the exception. Rationing was still in force, but there never seemed to be enough goods to satisfy all customers. At one stage the only bread available was yellow and made of maize meal.

Of course, we did not starve; we just had to adjust consumption to what was available. Occasionally we could buy shrimps and little flounders straight from the boats in the tiny harbour, which incidentally also served as the local swimming pool in summer. One of Opa's elderly friends taught me to fillet flatfish as professional chefs do it.

Although I now had an income again, there were few items of clothing to buy in the shops. However, the *Tauschzentrale*, a place where people could exchange unwanted items for something they needed, did a roaring business. I had few things that could be swapped for others, but was given some items occasionally. So I managed to acquire a much-needed pair of serviceable shoes for some balls of wool. A table lamp not in use was worth an army blanket, which could be turned into a coat.

Hairdressers did well at the time; even I spent some of my hard earned cash at Frau Mucha's place to acquire the latest hairstyle. Frau Mucha claimed to be a distant relative of the Viennese artist, Alphonse Mucha, of the Art Nouveau period and had decorated her salon with some of his posters.

I spent a substantial amount of money going to the one and only cinema in Varel, and must have seen every film while I was in town. I suppose it was an acceptable place for a single person to go. I did not know any people of my own age, nor had I relatives to be with or talk to. It was this that prompted Opa and his friends to suggest that I should be enrolled in a dancing class at Frau Behrens' studio. It was quite enjoyable to go there and join class members for a coffee afterwards, but I must have been a great disappointment to Heinz, my allocated dancing partner, when I did not respond to his declarations of affection. 'All this could be yours,' he said one evening when he accompanied me back to Elizabeth Street, showing me his substantial family home and business, which he would eventually inherit. He was a very kind man, but I was just not ready to enter into any closer relationships then.

In July 1947, when I heard that my parents and Karlheinz had been evicted from home and were living in Dresden, the Thorbeckes gave me time off to travel there to see them. This was easier said than done, because no official travel routes to the

Russian Zone existed then. I had heard that people did manage to cross the border stealthily, and I made contact with one of my former schoolmates who now lived in the Harz Mountains, where it was supposed to be not too difficult to find a path that led to East Germany.

I joined one or two other illegal travellers whom I had met on the train to my friend's place and we crept eastward along redundant railway lines through brushwood very early in the morning, hoping to evade any border guard on the way.

Needless to say, I heaved a sigh of relief when we reached the first railway station to catch a train to my destination, Dresden.

I found my parents and Karlheinz living in a single room, with my brother sleeping on the floor. The reunion was more than emotional, and once again we grieved for our lost home, and the idyllic life we had once led there. Still, we were glad to be alive and able at last to see each other again. We even drank a toast. Mother had found a job in a spirit factory and was being paid in 'kind'. Vodka was the main product, but essences were available to make liqueurs from the raw spirit. We had raspberry liqueur that evening to follow the stew made from *Dörrgemüse*, dried vegetables with potatoes. I had been able to bring some food supplies from Varel with me – most welcome as a little 'extra'. Father did some temporary work for a joiner in Hellerau, but was searching the area for a job in a bakery, which luckily soon came his way. The baker even had a couple of spare rooms, so the family could live on site.

My return journey to Varel brought its difficulties. I was apprehended by border guards near Nordhausen and taken to a fenced garden where a closer check on the rounded-up offenders was to be made. However, I found a gap in the fence behind some bushes and managed to abscond before my identity card had been confiscated. Once again, I crept through brushwood, not daring to look back or stop even when the uphill slope made me breathless. I just hoped that I had reached the Western Zone at the time I collapsed and just could not go any further.

When I recovered sufficiently to get going again it was dark, but I saw a glimmer of light in the valley below me. It could only be the village I was heading for – and I soon discovered that it was! There are no words to describe the relief I felt to be in safe territory again.

I stumbled on to the platform of the tiny train station and waited patiently, along with a few dozen other adventurers, for some sort of transport to appear. A few hours later I was on my way back to Varel and very glad to arrive there.

Herr Seller's Predictions

During the autumn of 1948 I heard on one of my frequent visits to the labour exchange that domestic workers were wanted in England. This seemed to be an opportunity not to be missed, since all attempts to find a more fulfilling job in Germany had eluded me. Working in England would at least help to broaden my horizons.

My application for inclusion to the North Sea Action scheme was successful, and in January 1949, I sailed to England.

Herr Seller's predictions came to mind once again, as they had done several times before – when crossing the River Neisse had almost become a habit. This time I would certainly cross bigger waters, and I hoped for plain sailing.

Herr Seller tended to strut around the village with his silver-knobbed walking stick. He had a neatly trimmed goatee beard and alert beady eyes behind gold-rimmed glasses. He prided himself on being psychic, able to foretell the future. He had a heavy gold watch on a long chain, usually suspended between his waistcoat pockets, but sometimes used as a pendulum, which circled and swung in various directions to indicate answers to questions he had in mind or which people asked him to answer.

I don't know how he did it. We often giggled about his eccentricity, but the laughter stopped when he rightly predicted that a war would start at the beginning of September 1939, and that Frau Keller would have twins before she herself knew that she was pregnant.

He also predicted earnestly that I would have to work very hard in my life to make a living and that I would cross the 'big waters' many times in years to come. This seemed to be a very odd forecast for a thirteen-year-old living in a totally landlocked village in Silesia, where the biggest expanse of water was the local swimming pool. There was, of course, also the River Queis, no more than twenty metres wide, which we had to cross every time we wished to go to the nearest village.

How could he possibly have known that I would end up living and working in England some years later, resulting in many subsequent sea crossings?

He said that it would not always be 'plain sailing'. There are certainly few happy memories attached to the first time I crossed the 'big water' – the English Channel – on my way to a new beginning. It was not a luxury liner or a streamlined ferry that brought me to England, but a clapped-out troop transporter, made redundant after the war.

Near to one hundred applicants like me were asked to report to a camp near Osnabruck in January 1949, and after interviews, medicals, prophylactic injections and signing of papers, we were dispatched to Hook of Holland, where our boat was waiting.

I don't know what I had expected, but the rusty hull of the transporter was not exactly confidence inspiring, neither were the swaying gangways nor the primitive hammocks in the hold, which were to be our sleeping accommodation for the night.

When the ship eventually left the harbour on that dark, damp January night I felt intensely alone in spite of fellow travellers milling around me, trying to get a last glimpse of mainland Europe as it receded into the distance. There had been few certainties for me during the past few years but the near future was even more daunting. Was this really the best way forward for me?

We had not been used to rich food in post-war Germany, and the Dutch sailors had made an effort to treat their temporary guests to a rounded meal in a harbour shack. We had eaten heartily and at the time truly enjoyed it, but the rich food was obviously not the best foundation for a rocky and emotion-laden sea journey.

It was not surprising then that the hold soon resembled a messy sickbay, from which I speedily escaped to spend most of the chilly night on deck, draped over the icy railing while being sick or sheltering in a wind-free recess near the boiler room, huddled in a sheet of oilskin. The sailors on deck had given this to me when I declined to join them in the primitive canteen area, where the smell of boiling milk and frying eggs added to my nausea.

ARBEITS-PASS

Nr. 1271409096 Personalausweis Nr. AQ/PDF 222810

Familienname: **KÖNIG**, Vorname: **Rosemarie**

geboren am **11.8.1927**

Geburtsort: **Kensdorf Kr. Lauban**

Familienstand: led.

Wohnung: **Varel,-Elisabethstr. 130**

Erlernter Beruf:

Berufs-Gruppe und -Art:

Beschäftigt als: **Hausgehilfin**

My last work permit in Germany

En route to England, January 1949

H GW 62/5

MILITARY GOVERNMENT FOR GERMANY
GOUVERNEMENT MILITAIRE POUR L'ALLEMAGNE
MILITÄRREGIERUNG FÜR DEUTSCHLAND

French — Français — Französisch
British — Anglais — Englisch
American — Américain — Amerikanisch

Temporary Travel Document
in lieu of passport
for German National

Titre de voyage provisoire
tenant lieu de passeport
pour personnes de nationalité allemande

Vorläufiger Reiseausweis
an Stelle eines Passes
für Deutsche Staatsangehörige

Number: 203472

HOLDER — TITULAIRE — INHABER

Name: **KÖNIG, ROSEMARIE**

This document contains 24 pages excluding the outer cover.
Ce document contient 24 pages, non compris la couverture.
Dieser Ausweis enthält 24 Seiten, die Umschlagseiten nicht mitgerechnet.

So I sat on a barrel, leaning against the lukewarm metal of the funnel, barely caring whether I lived or died. My face and hair were soon damp from the sea mist, and acrid fumes from the funnel drifted past when the boat or the wind changed direction. The swishing sounds of the waves drowned the moans from the hold and the clanking of utensils in the galley, but I could hear and feel the regular rhythm of the engines underfoot. From time to time the foghorn blew eerie warning signals into the inclement night.

I must have drifted off for a while from sheer exhaustion. When consciousness returned I was stiff all over and my feet felt like lumps of ice. Dawn was breaking and judging by the sound of multiple foghorns, the tinkling of bell buoys and the nearness of other vessels, we were close to the coast and our destination.

We reached Harwich at last; very cold and still feeling sick, and swaying on what was supposed to be solid ground.

Herr Seller's predictions came to mind. This crossing of the 'big water' had definitely not been 'plain sailing'. However, once I found my feet in England and proper passenger ferries came into operation, channel crossings became an almost pleasurable experience.

Part Four

A New Country and a New Start

First Impressions of England

January 1949

I had heard of English smog, but had not expected it to be as all-pervasive as it was on that January morning in Harwich. It seemed to blunt the senses: warning sounds came from nowhere and perspectives were distorted so that one could not get a full picture of the environment. The acrid smell in the damp air filled the lungs and affected the taste of the light-brown liquid that uniformed ladies offered us on arrival. It was supposed to be coffee, 'Camp Coffee', someone said.

When we were herded into a train for the next stage of our journey at last, the fog seemed to break up, swirling around us. Then the sky lightened as sunrays peeked through and gave us fleeting glimpses of stretches of green countryside, somewhat surprising after the sludgy snow we had left behind in Westphalia.

The next few days were spent in a Nissen hut camp in West Wratting near Cambridge, where we learned to appreciate English tea and English breakfasts as well as the comfort of a Cannon stove (a primitive and portable stove) in the middle of the hut. We huddled around it, draped in army blankets from our camp beds. It was quite cosy and helped us to begin to feel more at ease in England. We talked about our fears and disappointments, our hopes and aspirations. We were all in the same boat, so to speak. Lasting friendships were established at this time.

Large trestle tables had been set up in the dining hut where we were summoned after breakfast. Officials busied themselves with files, forms, lists and maps and eventually began the not-too-easy task of matching potential workers with available work.

We had no idea where we would end up, but all hoped to go to London, which had a certain glamorous ring to it or, maybe, to Brighton, which had figured in our reading exercises in school days. As it was, we were only given a choice of places in Scotland or in the Manchester region, where 'it always rains', according to one of the camp kitchen maids.

Since Scotland seemed even more remote and daunting, three of us, who had pledged to keep in touch with each other for mutual support, joined the queue for Manchester and were offered work in strange-sounding places like Crawshawbooth, Rawtenstall and Rochdale. We did not know what to expect, just heard that some householders lived there who had applied to employ a domestic help through this North Sea Action scheme.

England looked quite small on the map, so it came as a surprise that the train took six hours to reach the capital of the north-west, Manchester. The upholstery in our compartment was dusty and stained but quite comfortable, and the train was well heated – an absolute luxury after our experience on the boat. I drifted off to sleep for a while but woke up when more uniformed ladies on a platform offered cups of Camp Coffee.

It was foggy again but eventually the smog gave way to rain as the train steamed northward, skirting dingy-looking towns and passing through smoke-blackened stations. Even now I can readily recall the black dripping walls of Crewe station and the rows of little houses which flanked cobbled streets, without a tree, shrub or patch of grass in sight, grim and desolate. These depressing vistas and the fact that dusk was falling did not exactly raise our spirits and once again we wondered what we had let ourselves in for. It was almost like bereavement when the three of us had to part on reaching Manchester – to be ferried on to our final destinations: Castleton, Rochdale, in my case.

The Bridges' chauffeur-driven car picked me up and then made its way up the hilly approach to the main road. It was difficult to see the surroundings since acrid smog once again clouded the view.

'Don't worry, it's not always as bad as that,' Mrs Bridge said – a smartly dressed lady in a black fur coat and velvet hat.

'We will soon be home,' Mr Bridge added kindly. He was slightly built and somewhat bent, with wispy grey hair, a large nose and twinkling eyes – not exactly what I had imagined a big factory owner might look like.

'Rosemarie – that is a nice name,' he continued. 'We will call you Rose.' So I became Rose for the duration of my stay in the Bridge household.

The house was a large Victorian semi with stone steps leading up to an ornamental stained glass door. The panelled walls and thick carpets in the hall and on the staircase, as well as the gleaming antique furniture, exuded a feeling of richness. I did not realise at the time that it would fall to me to keep all this splendour polished and dust-free at all times as well as keeping the wide front door steps clear of dirt and scuff marks with the help of what Mrs Bridge called 'elbow grease', a scrubbing brush and a donkey stone.

I was ushered into the morning room next to the kitchen and offered a cup of tea and a biscuit while Finch, the chauffeur-cum-handyman-cum-gardener brought in my tatty suitcase, which looked somewhat out of place in these opulent surroundings. It looked much less conspicuous once in the attic room, which was to be my bedroom. This was clean enough but merely functional, with a large, old bed that occupied a quarter of the floor space, a rickety chair acting as bedside table, a small dressing table and half a wardrobe at my disposal – the other half being occupied by stacks of linen dating back to the time when Mrs Bridge had the notion of opening a hotel. She had eight children instead. There was a stack of rolled carpets at the end of the room and an old trunk, strong enough to stand on to reach the attic window, which had a lovely view over the house's large garden and the farmland beyond.

The only form of heating for me was a small one-bar electric fire, which barely warmed my knees when dressing. However, I was allowed to use two huge stoneware hot-water bottles to warm my bed on particularly cold nights. The room was obviously meant only as a place to retire to once the day's chores had been done, which was rarely before 10 p.m. My sitting room, if ever there was time to sit down, was to be the morning room. A small radio had been installed so that I could listen to the programmes of the day – *Mrs Dale's Diary*, *Family Favourites*, and so on – while ironing, cleaning the silver or darning socks when the bigger household tasks had been done.

I slept like the proverbial log on the first night – I can't even remember dreaming. Dreams in a strange bed, in a strange house, indeed, in a totally new life might have been significant to someone more superstitious than I am.

When the old-fashioned alarm clock with bells on top startled me back to reality the next morning I had to think for a minute to recall where I was, what had happened and had been said last night. Many impressions – both positive and negative – crowded my mind.

This was Sunday and therefore not a typical working day. I did not need to be downstairs before eight. Someone had lit the fire in the morning room and offered me a cup of tea, one of the very few which I was given. I became very proficient at tea making several times a day for different people, so it was not surprising that a quarter-pound tea bag did not last very long. Tea at home was nothing like the dark brown strong brew here. Fifty grams of tea lasted us for weeks. I was told that tea was still rationed in England, but good customers at the 'top shop' were treated generously.

One by one the family members appeared downstairs and had some cereals and toast while I poured never-ending cups of tea. Then they vanished to pursue their individual interests. Mr Bridge went to his brother who was a partner in the family firm and lived nearby. Mr David attended to his homing pigeons and Mr Arthur to his prize-winning corgis before going to the Christian Science Church, which he had taken to after one of his sisters died who had adopted that faith. Mr Wallace went to see his girlfriend, who modelled clothes at times. She seemed very sophisticated to me but apparently was not quite what 'Mother' had wanted for her youngest son.

That Sunday I was being introduced to the way the household was run and what was expected of me, which seemed to be an awful lot. Apparently before the war Mrs Bridge employed two full-time maids and also had part-time help. Anni, the part-time cleaner, was the last survivor of these employees, came in once or twice a week to do the 'rough' work like scrubbing the tiled floors in the kitchen, scullery and wash house and the flagged backyard. She also helped with the 'big' wash and occasionally did some spring-cleaning of rooms, which were not regularly 'turned out'.

There had not been a live-in maid for a year or so: I was considered to be the answer to Mrs Bridge's prayers. Anyway, that Sunday, I helped to cook the roast beef lunch and learned to set the table properly.

After midday the men drifted in one by one. Some had a glass of sherry, a drink I had never heard of before, while Mrs Bridge made the gravy and the Yorkshire pudding, which was not like any pudding I had ever eaten. I spent some time whipping artificial cream for the trifle. There was a hatch to the dining room through which I passed the prepared dishes for the family.

I ate in the morning room and actually found this quite relaxing after a morning of questions and instructions that made me more panic-stricken by the moment. How on earth could I live up to all these expectations?

Mr Bridge eventually had a nap in front of the sitting room fire in his favourite chair from where he could stoke the embers from time to time, putting another log of wood or lump of coal on. He loved to have the odd cigar but had to wait till his wife had left the room. She went upstairs to lie down and rest after the exertions of the morning and the 'boys', aged between twenty-eight and thirty-eight, went off to do their own things again. I cleared the dishes, washed up and pegged the rinsed tea towel out on the line in the yard as instructed, before sinking exhaustedly into the old but comfortable easy chair in the morning room to listen to the radio, drifting off into oblivion myself until the bell reminded me that Madam was ready for her afternoon tea.

During the afternoon, more family members appeared to inspect me as the new arrival. Mrs Fletcher lived next door with her two young teenagers. Her husband was not welcome in the Bridges' house for some reason. Mr Jack, another son, who lived nearby and also worked in the family firm brought his wife and 'young David' (nine) and 'little George' to see me. I had plenty of opportunity to try out my school-taught English, but soon realised that while I was easily understood, I had difficulties in making out what had been said. It became better after I asked them to try to talk to me one at a time and to speak slowly and clearly. They tried hard to do so. Everyone wanted to know about my background and the tortuous journey that brought me to

England and to Rochdale in particular. 'I quite like you,' Jonathan from next door said eventually. 'You will be able to help me with my German homework.'

Was I glad when the 'Salad Tea' was over and the kitchen had once more been cleared!

'You look tired,' Mr Bridge said perceptively. 'Mother says you can have an early night.' I needed no further prompting to drag myself to my attic, and even forgot the hot-water bottles.

Establishing Routines

When the alarm clock woke me at 6.30 the next morning, I threw my clothes on speedily to get out of my freezing attic and into an only slightly less chilly morning room, where my first task was to light the fire. To my surprise I actually managed to do this, once I had raked the ashes from the grate of the marble fireplace, saving bits of coal that had not totally burned out, as instructed. Finch had left a bucket of coal and some kindling in the porch outside the kitchen and had advised me to use plenty of crumpled-up newspaper to get the fire going. It soon began to add some warmth and cheer to the gloomy morning.

Having no access to the bathroom at that time of the day, I scrubbed my black hands, washed my face and cleaned my teeth in the wash house behind the kitchen before putting the kettle on for the first brew of the day. Soon after, the 'boys' had their cups of tea in bed. Then it was Mr and Mrs Bridge's turn to have their wake-up beverage in a small silver teapot on a silvery tray set with dainty bone china cups and two plain biscuits. Their bedroom was the most opulent in the house, all cream, pink and gilt. I was told on numerous occasions that the ornate furniture was made of bleached mahogany by Waring and Gillows and that the thick, pale velour carpet had been made to order in a Yorkshire mill. My attic was a far cry from this room but then I was only the hired hand and glad to simply have a roof over my head and the chance to earn my own living, although I was beginning to realise that I had not chosen an easy option.

By 7.45, the men of the house were up and having their breakfast – just cereals and toast and more tea. They came home for a cooked lunch at midday. The factory was only a mile or so away and Finch was available to drive them there and back on request.

While having her breakfast in bed, Madam gave me the in-structions for the day. The first task was to wash and prepare the vegetables for lunch, so that she could get on with the cooking later while I did whatever cleaning was to be done that day. It was imperative that the front door steps were spotless at all times, the hall and sitting room dusted and vacuumed, and two fires kept burning throughout the day.

Apart from these routine tasks I was supposed to turn out all occupied rooms in the house in strict rotation. I really could not see the reason for pulling out beds and chests of drawers every week or two, and dusting picture rails, walls and lamp fittings. These were things that we would have done at home only at spring-cleaning times or for special occasions. I soon learned to cut corners when I was left alone with my task to save time, energy and my sanity. Nobody seemed to note the difference! I panicked once, when in my haste to get another room finished I chipped some varnish off the skirting board, exposing bare wood in a most obvious place. Luckily, by then, I had found out where the gravy brown and the boot polish were kept, which camouflaged the damage most effectively.

Cooking lunch tended to leave madam totally exhausted and ready for a rest, while I continued with my seemingly never-ending chores and eventually started preparations for high tea. This was not usually a big meal unless there were visitors in the house. It often consisted of fairly plain salads with slices of cold meat. Sometimes we had grated cheese, melted under the grill in ramekins, or boiled onions eaten with pepper, salt and butter. All of these were offered with plenty of fluffy white bread, quite unlike the coarse rye bread I was used to. Cakes, scones and biscuits were popular with the men and also with me to start with, not having been used to such luxuries.

At bedtime more tea was brewed. Mr Bridge particularly liked some cheese with crackers at that time of day. Never having seen foreign cheeses before, I decided one evening that the Roquefort looked distinctly unsavoury and discarded it because, as I later explained I had thought that the cheese 'was not very well'. This was the first time that I heard Mrs Bridge laugh as she joined in with the others. For some reason I never lived this episode down. It was inevitably brought up when cheeses were served, and used to entertain guests with. In later years, when the Bridges came to my own home for a meal, comments were still made about the quality of the cheeses and their fitness for consumption. 'Aye, Rose, the cheese is well today,' old Mr Bridge would say with a chuckle, and everybody would join in the laughter.

Spreading my Wings

Days and weeks at 1070 Manchester Road passed fast, giving little time for boredom or reflection. I missed some friends in Germany, but homesickness was not an issue since I had no proper home to go to anyway. I knew that my parents and brothers were struggling themselves to re-establish their existence.

Domestic routines soon became familiar and I began to spread my wings. I became known to the sales assistants at the 'top shop' – so-called because it stood at the top of an incline, not because it was superior in any way. A weekly order was placed there, but a fair lot of casual shopping was done in-between. Even organised households like that of the Bridges' ran out of salt occasionally or needed extra bread to cater for unexpected visitors.

The shop owner's had been a soldier in Germany and liked to show off his language skills. He also tipped me off when a rare consignment of custard powder or Nescafé had come in. The fishmonger knew that Mrs Bridge was very particular about the way her fish was filleted and that she liked a lot of fresh parsley. The greengrocer was aware of the size of carrots or potatoes she preferred. Meat was delivered to the house by a stout, red-faced man in a cloth cap and a striped butcher's apron. He called me 'blossom' and expected a cup of tea if there was one going. Strangely enough Mrs Bridge did not object to this. I suspect she got somewhat preferential treatment – more generous rations than the coupons allowed. I was rather surprised that coupons were still in use for some commodities. My first sweet coupons were spent on a Caley Milk Tray – six fancy pralines joined together on a milk chocolate base, beautifully wrapped – absolute luxury to me.

I noticed the swimming bath next to the sweet shop and discovered that for a small sum one could use the 'slipper baths' with almost unlimited amounts of hot water and a clean towel provided. I made use of that facility on some of my afternoons off, finding the five inches of water I was allowed to use in the Bridge household on a Tuesday afternoon, when none of the men were in the house, rather limited.

Rochdale was a twenty-minute bus ride away and the next target for exploration. There I found the most interesting market I had ever been to. I stared in wonder at the plethora of goods for sale, not only in the food hall but also on the outdoor stalls: shoes of all descriptions, handbags, underwear and outerwear, coats and even hats and stockings, which were almost unobtainable in Germany. Markets I had known at home tended to be the preserve of local farmers, who sold eggs and other farm and garden produce at them.

Overwhelmed by my new experiences and footsore from all the walking, I decided to have some refreshment in the smart-looking Bonbon Cafe nearby. I felt quite sophisticated when placing my order and having tea served to me in a silver teapot, accompanied by a crystal plate with six cakes on it. By the time I had eaten an éclair, a little coconut pyramid and a small apple pie, I felt truly satisfied and apologised to the waitress that, although the cakes were really delicious, I could not possibly eat any more. Ignorant of prevailing customs, I did not know that they were presented for me to choose one or two from, not for the consumption of the whole lot. I became quite friendly with the waitresses and the Bonbon Cafe became a meeting place when my compatriots from Rawtenstall and Crawshawbooth joined me in Rochdale.

One of the two huge cinemas in the centre of town provided entertainment for the rest of the afternoon and evening. Several films would be shown each day and, once in the auditorium, one could stay for as long as one wanted for the same entrance price. I was very impressed with the first film I saw in England – *The Red Shoes*, which is still shown occasionally these days, many years later. It always reminds me of my first momentous outing to Rochdale.

I got to know Manchester too in due course when Mrs Bridge sent me there to do some errands, like buying what she thought were rather exotic foods in the only delicatessen in the centre.

Only initiates seemed to know of Brumme's, a quaint little shop in a backyard off Corporation Street, where continental salads, breads, cheeses and sausages could be bought. The scents and sights reminded me very much of home.

Another time I had to take Mrs Bridge's furs to Kendals for cleaning and summer storage. I felt quite insecure in the opulent fur department, but must have looked sufficiently sophisticated in my grey swagger coat and matching hat (from the market!), because while one assistant dealt with the furs another offered to show 'Madam' the latest mink collection. I pleaded lack of time, barely able to prevent myself from giggling at the thought of me being considered capable of purchasing luxury items. Still, that incident boosted my confidence considerably. Perhaps Mrs Bridge's idea of not ever going out unless properly attired with hat and gloves was not so silly after all.

Mrs Bridge's perpetual health problems stopped her walking very far, so she relied on Finch to drive her to her destinations. Since he was not always available when she wanted to go out, she decided that I must learn to drive. I was duly enrolled for a course of lessons at the Rochdale School of Motoring and was given additional driving practice by Finch at weekends. This widened my horizons considerably. I learned starting, straight driving and stopping on the shores of Hollingworth Lake, hill starts on Blackstone Edge, and reversing and three-point turns – often more like seven-point turns – in the backstreets behind the station. I passed my test at the first attempt on a slushy December day in Bolton.

It took some time before Madam trusted me and the small Ford I was allowed to drive, but I gained experience through collecting whale meat and National Dried Milk from a supplier, which Mr Arthur fed to his prize-winning corgis. Mr Bridge made me drive the Razor Edge to his wine merchant once, very much against his wife's better judgement. I am still not sure if it was me driving her big car or the alcoholic purchases she objected to. 'Mother is in a bad mood today,' Mr Bridge observed, when I seemed ill at ease. 'She will calm down. I can't let her always get her way.' She had actually made some tea for us when we returned, all in one piece, with a couple of crates of wine and whisky in the boot.

On New Year's Day I revisited Bolton. Mr Arthur had entered one of his corgis in a dog show, but was too ill to take the animal there himself. He considered me to be capable of doing this for him and, although totally inexperienced in this field, I was persuaded to go.

'Daleviz Junior' behaved himself well in the car but wanted to escape the moment I found a parking space. I just about caught him and decided to carry him to the show venue, so that his paws would not get wet or dirty. I was not at all sure what I was doing but followed the exhibitor in front of me through the procedures: general assessment, health and weight checks, and measuring of the tails. Corgies are supposed to have only a stump of a tail. Eventually we were allotted a small booth, next to a lady with a miniature poodle, which had pink bows on his head. Having tethered Daleviz to a provided hook I set out to find a fellow dog breeder who had agreed to parade the dog in front of the judges when the corgi category came up. We actually came home with the label 'Highly Commended' which sounded better to me than just a prize. Daleviz Junior was eventually sold abroad and became the Canadian champion.

Miss Lord from the labour exchange came from time to time to assess my situation. I had to get the best china cups out, buy a Battenberg cake and use the solid silver teapot (newly polished, of course) to impress the inspector. Although I rarely seemed to please Madam, she told Miss Lord that she was totally satisfied with me and that I fitted well into the household. Visiting me in the kitchen later, Miss Lord asked what I was going to do with my holidays, since I had no one to go to in England. Mrs Bridge had never mentioned before that I was entitled to two weeks' paid holidays per annum, although she had grudgingly given me the odd day off when I told her that my compatriots from Rawtenstall had asked me to join them on day trips to Blackpool, Morecambe and later Llandudno.

We thought Blackpool was fascinating and enjoyed lounging on the beach and mingling with the crowds on the promenade, licking ice cream and eating fish and chips with salt and vinegar from folds of newspaper, which Madam would have found very common.

We did not like Morecambe as much but enjoyed the bathing belle contest at the lido, with a kind of water ballet to follow. We felt very sophisticated having a shandy when the coach stopped at a country pub on the way back to Manchester.

On my first year in England I decided to spend a week's holiday at Butlins Holiday Camp in North Wales. Madam thought a Christian group walking holiday would be preferable to a free and easy place like Butlins, where a young woman might be exposed to all sorts of sinful temptations. Still, I did go to Butlins, but my sinful activities amounted to no more than a chaste kiss and cuddle behind the chalet when Barry from Nottingham took me back there after we had danced together all evening.

Apart from the rousing morning calls over a really noisy loudspeaker I quite enjoyed the hustle and bustle of organised activities – swimming, dancing, talent contests, films and evening entertainments. Huge, tasty meals were served in big dining halls. The fact that I did not have to prepare them and clear up afterwards made them even more acceptable. I did not miss other daily chores either: 'stoning' the steps and constantly being at Madam's beck and call. I got on well with Hilary, from London, with whom I shared a chalet. We walked along the coast one day when we came to a little private airfield, where two men were getting their small light aircraft ready for take-off. Noting our interest, they asked if we fancied going for a spin. The offer was too good to refuse and in no time we had our first unexpected flying experience, sweeping over the North Wales coast and the hills beyond. We offered to buy them lunch as a thank you gesture, but they declined, saying that they were rewarded enough by having the opportunity to show off their newly acquired flying skills to two charming enthusiasts. This was definitely the high light of our camp week!

The year after, I had a more sophisticated holiday. I had discovered the Batty-Holt travel agency near the driving school and found that for less than a couple of months' wages I could book a coach tour of the south coast and London.

This would be the ideal opportunity to see a little more of England before my contract expired. I knew it would not be easy to pay for it, but I was not an extravagant spender and could cut down a bit on the parcels I sent regularly to my parents in East Germany. The holiday wardrobe could be fashioned out of cheap remnants from the market.

It was quite exciting to travel through a substantial part of England in a luxury coach and in the company of very friendly and congenial fellow travellers.

I loved Devon and Cornwall, especially the quaint little fishing villages. I ate my first ever lobster in Newquay, had cream teas in thatched cottages and midnight swims in Paignton. Bournemouth seemed grand and elegant compared with Blackpool.

The hotel we stayed at in London, in a leafy street in Kensington was not big but had a rather select clientele. It must have been around 12 August when the retired laird from Scotland educated me about grouse shooting. The grouse served for dinner that night was quite tasty but on the bony side. I could not see what all the fuss was about; neither could the deposed baron from Latvia, who had been used to deer hunting on his estate. He seemed to enjoy talking to me in German, and even bought me a glass of claret to go with the grouse. Rochdale seemed very far away then.

London was amazing. On my first day there, the palatial buildings and shops, historical sites and bustling streets bowled me over. I could scarcely believe that I myself was experiencing what we had read about in English lessons at college, like 'Bill and Betty walked over Westminster Bridge when Big Ben struck ten.' The day after we made a boat trip on the Thames from the Houses of Parliament to Tower Bridge. A visit to 'Dirty Dick's Pub' in the East End followed. There was just time to find a few little bargains on Petticoat Lane market before the coach set off for the north and back to reality.

My fellow travellers spoiled me and felt quite protective to-wards me – a young woman travelling alone, living and working in England with no family to fall back on. Before we parted in Manchester several invitations to visit families in Bolton, Northwich and other places, had been issued, but I never found the time to follow up these invitations.

Bill Grundy from St Helen's said in passing 'You are wasted as a skivvy in Rochdale.' I was beginning to think so myself and resolved to leave the Bridges the moment my contract expired.

Miss Lord had told me that I would be eligible to take up a limited range of other work after that, seeing as I had proved myself. Nursing was one of these options. Some inquiries led to an interview at Park Hospital in Davyhulme, a pleasant suburb of Manchester.

Before I returned to Germany two years after my arrival in England I knew that I would be able to come back to start training to be a nurse – providing that the hospital could gain an alien work permit for me.

GM

MINISTRY OF LABOUR AND NATIONAL SERVICE,

Foreign Labour Division,
1/2 Cumberland Terrace,
Regent's Park,
London, N.W.1.

PERMIT

under Article 1(3)(b) of

THE ALIENS ORDER, 1920

No. of Permit	Date of Issue	Period covered by permit _____twelve_____months from the date of landing in the United Kingdom.
145674	21 MAR 1951	

Employer's Name and Address.	Alien's Name, etc.
THE MATRON,	Surname _____KONIG,_____
PARK HOSPITAL,	Other Names ____Anna Ida Rosemarie____
DAVYHULME,	Date of Birth ____14th August, 1927____
NR. MANCHESTER	Sex ___Female___ Nationality ___German___
	Employment ___Student Nurse___
	T.1

...d employer subject to the conditions shown below :—

...G THE ISSUE OF THIS PERMIT

...ns. Siehe Rueckseite.]

A 243624

Aliens Order, 1920.

CERTIFICATE OF REGISTRATION

You must produce this certificate if required to do so by any Police Officer, Immigration Officer, or member of His Majesty's forces acting in the course of his duty.

...of his
...] Act
...ssport
...er or
...r for
...United

...ntrol
...date
...rt of
...er the

...n on
... visa,
...n the
...ill be
... that
...Aliens

...ration
...rdom.
...on for
...n.
...parti-
...avalid.

7. This permit is valid only for the particular employment for which it is issued and not for employment of another kind or with another employer.

8. The alien during the period of stay in the United Kingdom is subject to the restrictions, and must conform to the requirements, of the Aliens Order, 1920. If the permit is for a period of more than two months the alien is advised to be in possession of two additional copies of the photograph taken for passport purposes, for use when registering under the Aliens Order 1920.

9. If it is desired to employ the alien beyond the terminal date of the period for which the alien has been granted leave to land by the Immigration Officer, application should be made by the employer about one month before such date to the Under-Secretary of State, Home Office, Aliens Department, 271-7, High Holborn, London, W.C.1, marking the envelope in the bottom left-hand corner "M.L. Permit." The alien's passport should be forwarded with the application.

...behalf of the Minister of Labour and National Service

(signature)

After its number and date of issue have been noted this permit of four pages should be sent intact to the alien, who will be required to produce it to the Immigration Officer at the Port of arrival.

A.R.2.

9850) Wt 27882 2557 10M 11/50 CN&Co 789 (9574)

Work permit, 1951

Back to England

April 1951

My second trip to England was a definite improvement on the first one two years before. This time there were no hammocks in the hold or rusty chimneys to lean on, draped in tarpaulins to ward off the sea spray.

The old troop transporter had probably been taken out of service, making room for a regular ferry service to England on very comfortable boats. Not having been overfed on rich Dutch foods this time I was not sick either. In fact, I was hungry but nevertheless comfortable and pleased to be at last on my way to what I hoped would be a fulfilling future.

I could not afford a cabin or even a bunk but enjoyed the luxury of a well-upholstered armchair in the lounge. The seven-hour sea crossing gave plenty of time to reflect on the events of the last months and particularly on the trials and tribulations of the last twenty-four hours.

I had returned to Germany from Rochdale when my two-year work contract expired. I had been given to understand that I would be permitted to return to England to work in certain areas of employment if I could secure a place. The matron of Park Hospital had accepted me as a student nurse on a course starting at the beginning of April 1951.

Well over two months seemed to give ample time to acquire the appropriate papers: a new travel document, a work offer in writing, an alien work permit from the Ministry of Labour and National Service in London and, of course, the necessary travel visas.

I also wanted to catch up with friends and family members whom I had not seen for years. What I had not reckoned upon was that official wheels ground very slowly in England and that German efficiency, once taken for granted, had yet to be re-established. It took longer than anticipated to get a passport and even longer to get an Inter-zonal permit to visit my parents who, after expulsion from Silesia, were trying to establish a new existence in Dresden in the Russian Zone which was soon to be renamed DDR, Deutsche Demokratische Republik.

When I returned from that emotional trip at last, I had expected to find the alien work permit from London at my friend's address so that I could make my travel arrangements to England in time for the start of my course. Alas, no papers awaited me and no one seemed able to hasten the process.

Phone inquiries, if ever I managed to get through to an official place, only produced negative responses:

'You will have to wait your turn.'

'You can't apply for an entrance visa to England until your alien permit is at hand.'

'There is no point in applying for a Dutch transit visa until you have got the entrance visa for England.'

I just had to be patient and rely for rather longer than anticipated on the kindness of friends, for a roof over my head and invitations to meals to conserve my ever-dwindling resources. There were no more tins of Nescafé left to trade on the black market. I suppose I had been lucky to have a boxful of that desirable commodity to sustain me through poverty-stricken days in the first place.

I knew that the amount of coffee which could be sent in parcels abroad was limited to half a pound, but had not realised that the same rules applied to goods to be taken personally out of the country for one's own consumption or as presents – or in my case, as bartering objects.

So when departure from Castleton approached, I had hoarded a boxful of Nescafé tins, which had become available for sale in England when stocks could be found. My friend at the top shop had alerted me when a new consignment had arrived. I knew that the stuff would be very much appreciated by the coffee-loving Germans after years of deprivation on grain coffee and chicory substitutes. I had heard that a small tin was worth six marks, which would go some way to repay my friend's hospitality.

When the train approached the Dutch/German border after

the channel crossing, we were ordered to leave the train and present ourselves for passport and luggage checks at the Customs Office. We had to carry our baggage, and in the absence of porters I found it difficult to handle my suitcase and handbag, never mind the cardboard box full of tins. Reluctantly I left it behind under the seat, saying a sad goodbye to my treasure trove.

The queue moved slowly as officials checked our papers and belongings very thoroughly, resulting in the confiscation of any items, including coffee, tea and chocolates, and certainly alcohol, considered to be 'over the limit'. I consoled myself with the thought that I would have lost my coffee anyway if I had been able to drag it along with me.

After this ordeal we waited on the freezing platform to continue our journey. The train, which puffed eventually into the station, was the same one that had carried us before. We were herded into the carriages, and there were more people than places on the train. I managed to get back into coach N, where to my surprise the box still stood under the seat where I had left it.

I had to change trains in Osnabruck, from where I had departed two years before for my new life in England. This time Varel in Oldenburg was my destination. In the absence of a proper home address my ticket was made out to my last place of residence in Germany, where friends and former employers had kindly offered accommodation for the time needed to obtain the necessary papers and permits to enable me to return to work in England.

Only a few days were left before the start of the nursing course when, at long last, my alien work permit arrived from London. If I wanted to reach Manchester in the near future I had no option but to travel in person to the consulates in Hamburg to obtain my visas. Postal applications would take too long.

Luckily, I had a friend in Hamburg who offered me overnight accommodation in her flat and who knew her way around the city, so that getting my paperwork sorted out took only one day. Visa fees and the cost of this emergency trip made a big hole in my savings. Elizabeth, whom I had met in Rochdale and who had gone back to her hometown to work, lent me fifty marks and insisted on showing me the *Reeperbahn*, the entertainment quarter of the port area, before depositing me on the night train back to Osnabruck and Varel.

At last I could embark on my trip to England with a trunk which contained all my worldly possessions and a hundred marks, half of them borrowed, which I naively thought would see me through to my destination: Park Hospital, Davyhulme, Manchester. This time I had to finance my travels myself.

'A one-way ticket to Manchester, via Hook of Holland, Harwich and London,' the man at the ticket office in Osnabruck said. 'That will be ninety-seven marks fifty on the boat train. Of course, you will have to pay separate for the luggage, your case is too big to take into the compartment.'

What now? The boat train was leaving in about two hours. Where could I procure at least fifteen marks to continue my journey? There was no time to contact friends in Varel and I knew no one in Osnabruck. Loan facilities and credit cards did not exist then.

I had to part with four silver coins that had survived the Russian onslaught camouflaged as coat buttons. Mother had maintained that I should keep them as an iron reserve. There was no time to find a coin dealer in this strange town within the limited time I had. A man in a jewellery shop was only prepared to offer ten marks for the coins, which I reluctantly accepted. The only other item of any value in my possession was a gold chain with an amethyst pendant, given to me by my godmother on my confirmation. I just could not bring myself to part with it for the mere ten marks which the man offered even if it would have breached the gap in my financial dilemma.

Then I racked my brain to find a solution and remembered the three pairs of stockings I had, which were then quite desirable objects in post-war Germany. Mother had given them to me on my recent visit to Dresden. A litre of vodka had paid for said stockings.

It seemed inappropriate to hawk my wares in the main station hall, so I tried my luck in the Ladies' toilet – only to be shown the door by the attendant. I must have looked quite harassed when I tried to peddle my wares in the adjoining block of flats. Was I glad when I found an interested buyer on the third floor. I parted with my treasured stockings for the princely sum of ten marks, an absolute bargain for her in black market terms, but it felt like a lifesaver for me.

There was only just time to get my ticket, pay for the carriage of my trunk, which the luggage handlers had kindly minded in my absence, and flop on to the first seat I could find on the boat train, utterly exhausted but triumphant that I had made it so far.

Passport and custom controls were dealt with smoothly as we speeded through Holland and eventually boarded the smart Dutch ferry. I was hungry and thirsty and felt tempted to spend all of the few marks I had left, but I settled for lemonade and a packet of crisps, which were the cheapest things to be had.

More problems came to mind when I looked at my ticket more closely and it dawned on me that I would have to change stations in London since the train arrived at Liverpool Street while the Manchester train departed from Euston. I had sixpence left from my Rochdale days, which would take me to the hospital site, but definitely not on a ride through London. Eventually a kind soul offered to take me along in her taxi and even offered to lend me ten shillings, which I reluctantly accepted and promptly repaid from my first earnings.

With some trepidation I sat on the number twenty-three bus on the way to Park Hospital towards another momentous episode of my life.

'You are too late,' Miss Dolan, the hospital matron, said, sitting stately and starched behind her impressive desk. 'The course started ten days ago. You will never be able to catch up with the rest.'

However, since my work permit specified that I was allowed to come to England for this course and no other employment, I was given the chance to try my best. I had nowhere else to go anyway.

It was heaven to be given a comfortable room of my own, to have unlimited baths available at the end of the corridor and regular meals provided in the nurses' dining room.

It was just as well that my penniless state did not permit me to join my fellow students on trips to the market or the cinema once the classroom work was done. I had a lot of theoretical knowledge to catch up on and spent every available hour copying notes the others had made during the intensive study programme, trying to make sense of the new terminology. After my two housemaid years I was quite comfortable with everyday English, but had never come across gallipots and Cheatle forceps, unguents and phenol derivatives and their dilution ratios, never mind the anatomical terms that never ceased to amaze me, like synovial membranes, or distal phalanges, which are actually toe bones.

While work was challenging and at times almost incomprehensible I enjoyed doing something positive. At the end of the three-month introductory course I passed my exam with flying colours and was able to begin my practical ward experience.

By then I had also paid off all my debts and felt again in control of my life.

Nursing Days

Once the introductory course and its associated exams were over, it was time to face reality. I was looking forward to going on to a ward and putting theory into practice, but made my way to ward three feeling a mixture of apprehension and excitement. It was a female medical ward with a Sister who had a reputation for being a bit of a slave-driver. She actually made me very welcome and asked Nurse Owen, a third-year nurse, to take me under her wing and introduce me to the ward routines. A procedure book was kept in the office, which was to be strictly followed.

If by then any notions were left that nursing consisted mainly of mopping fevered brows, holding patients' hands, administering important medicines or carrying out life-saving procedures, they were soon dispelled. It was domestic and basic hygiene concerns that dominated the day of a junior nurse.

The night shift had already made the beds and served breakfast when the day shift started at eight. Once the breakfast dishes had been taken away, we started to clean the ward. Wards in the 1950s were of the Nightingale type, i.e. large open spaces with beds lined up against the walls on either side and just a few cubicles and side rooms for patients who needed to be isolated or who required close observation or frequent attention. Occasionally private patients who were able and willing to pay for a measure of privacy occupied these spaces.

Every day all beds were pulled away from the walls to allow windowsills, radiators and skirting boards to be 'damp dusted'. Then used tea leaves or damp sawdust were scattered on the floor to gather the dust and fluff which tended to accumulate over the day and that had to be swept up regularly. Of course, vacuum cleaners eventually put an end to this quaint practice, which was actually quite efficient. We then had to make sure that the beds were pushed back exactly into their proper space at equal distance to their neighbours, with brakes applied and wheels turned inward at a forty-five degree angle to avoid stubbing of toes and tripping over.

I liked cleaning the patients' lockers. It gave me a chance to talk with them and get to know them better as individuals. Cards, pictures or fruit on the locker top often were the starting point of a conversation. However, idle chat tended to be frowned upon at other times and could give rise to reprimands by the Sister or Staff Nurse: 'Have you nothing better to do, Nurse?'

There were regular bedpan rounds for the patients' convenience, but in spite of that, work was sometimes interrupted by a frantic call for the 'pan'. I soon realised that it was expedient to answer such calls speedily since dealing with soiled beds and anxious and embarrassed patients later was much more time-consuming. The patients certainly seemed to appreciate the speed with which I tried to meet their needs. In one of the wards I worked on, a group of patients jocularly awarded me the title 'The Lady of the Loo'. It made me blush but I felt quite proud of it and joined in the ensuing laughter.

The sluice room had to be cleaned and tidied as well and bedpans, bottles and specimen jars washed and disinfected and stored on racks, ready for reuse. Disposable items and gadgets like automatic bedpan washers had yet to be introduced.

The ward had to be shipshape by 10 a.m. when Matron or her deputy made their daily tour of inspection. On other days the medical consultants and their entourages did their rounds as well. Sister joined them, pad and pen in her hand to note down comments and care suggestions. A senior nurse had to stand by to fetch and carry charts, X-rays and laboratory reports as requested. It all looked very important to me.

Apart from cleaning, junior nurses spent most of their time on general patient care: giving baths in the bathroom to those who could get up, and bed baths to the non-ambulant. Mouth care was seen to be important as was the treatment of pressure areas, to prevent bedsores caused by lack of blood flow to compressed areas. We seemed to be forever massaging areas like the sacrum, shoulder blades, elbows and heels, all of which were particularly vulnerable. It was almost seen to be a crime for patients to develop bedsores, and the least little graze or abrasion needed to be reported.

I was proud when I was allowed to begin to take temperatures, make poultices and give inhalations and enemas.

I will never forget the first injection I gave. Human skin and flesh definitely feel different from the oranges we had been given in the school to practise on. Staff Nurse wisely chose an unconscious patient for me to administer a penicillin injection to, and seemed to approve of my technique. Plenty of injection practice was available at the time since the recently introduced antibiotics penicillin and streptomycin were all the rage, but, to be fully effective, they had to be given every four hours, including night-time.

Only senior nurses were allowed to handle and dispense prescription pills and potions, especially those medicines which were on the poison register, but I was sometimes entrusted with giving of 'opening medicine' to needy patients, which one day led to a calamity. Syrup of figs, liquid paraffin and cascara each came in large two litre bottles. To save time I put them on a tray, along with some medicine glasses, on a mobile washstand, the only available conveyance at the time, and wheeled it around in search of customers – of which there were plenty. Then one of the wheels of the trolley ceased to turn while I was pushing, resulting in the whole lot being tipped over. Smashed glass mixed with litres of syrup of figs and the other oily concoctions made an awesome sight to behold. I froze in horror, dreading to report the mishap to Sister, fully expecting dismissal or at least a dreaded report to Matron. I was therefore more than surprised when, on surveying the scene, she started to roar with laughter and told me that cleaning up the mess would be ample punishment for me, as indeed it was. It took me hours, several buckets of sand, gallons of detergent and elbow grease to shift the debris and leave the floor in a fit state to walk on.

Surgery

New challenges faced me when I was allocated to a surgical ward. As a comparative newcomer I was mainly dealing with patients whose operations were pre-planned. I had to make sure that they had been seen by the 'house man', just to make sure that they were fit to be given an anaesthetic and that they had signed their consent form for the procedure.

The patients needed to be aware that no food or drink could be taken for several hours before going to theatre. Urine was tested for any abnormalities and an enema given to empty the bowels. The skin near the incision area had to be shaved and cleaned and painted with aseptic lotions before covering it with sterile towels. Before the patient was wheeled to the theatre a 'pre-med' was given, an injection of calming and relaxing drugs to induce drowsiness.

I will never forget the first time I took a patient to theatre. Once the outer doors closed new rules applied. I had to don a protective gown, cover my hair and wear a mask before entering the inner sanctum. A smell of antiseptic permeated the warm, moist air and bright lights illuminated the operating table, the gleaming stainless steel instruments, bowls and gallipots, as well as an array of machinery, gas and oxygen cylinders, suction pumps, drips and drainage bottles, standing by in case they were needed.

The first operation I witnessed was a partial gastrectomy, the removal of part of a stomach. It may have been a dramatic event for me, but it was just a routine procedure for the anaesthetist, the surgeons and the Sister. Everyone was dressed in green sterile gowns and caps, only eyes peeping over face masks. Of the patient only the operation site was exposed, painted yellow with iodine.

Everything proceeded smoothly and, contrary to initial fears, I did not faint when the first incision was made, exposing layers of skin, fat and muscle, accompanied by the smell of burning flesh when small blood vessels were sealed with a diathermy needle. Larger vessels were clamped and tied off. Little talking was done, other than the surgeons' requests for implements from the instrument trolley. 'Retractor' – 'Clamp' – 'Swab' – 'Suction' – 'Suture', etc. The Sister who was helping knew exactly what was wanted.

Eventually a receiver with a lump of removed tissue was handed to me who was acting as a runner, i.e. someone available to fetch and carry things, position drain and drip stands and help to count the swabs before the wound was closed – to make sure all were accounted for. There were no special recovery rooms at the time, but I had to wait for the anaesthetist to give clearance for the patient's return to the ward, where a special bed had been prepared for the aftercare. We had no sophisticated monitoring equipment, but relied on close observations and checking of pulse and breathing rates to assure us that the patient was not in shock and deteriorating, but was gradually recovering from his ordeal.

In the post-operative period, prevention of infections was high on the list of priorities. We had to use a non-touch technique to look after the wounds – that is, handle dressings, swabs, probes and drains, clips and stitches with forceps. Every item of equipment had to be sterile – even scrubbed hands were not considered to be safe enough. The tank in the clinic room was constantly bubbling away, boiling instruments, bowls, glassware and syringes in use. An over-keen nurse once even boiled the fever thermometers up to make them germ free. It was quite difficult to rid the steriliser of the mercury globules that had burst out of their glass casing.

We spent any free moments we had in the linen room, rolling cotton wool swabs, folding gauze dressings and gamgee pads as well as dressing towels and packing them into metal drums to be steam– and heat-sterilised in a central autoclave.

Things have changed a great deal since then: pre-sterilised and disposable materials make nurses' lives easier and, in theory at least, improve patient care; but there is still no substitute for the personal commitment by nurses to their patients to help them recover.

Mr Cornstein

It was on one of the surgical wards that I met Mr Cornstein. He had been placed in a cubicle, since his wailing, moaning and shouting in a foreign language disturbed the other patients. He was seen to be a troublemaker, certainly difficult to handle and thus to be avoided if at all possible, unless essential prescribed treatment was due. All that was known about him was that he had recently arrived in England from Russia and that neither he nor his diminutive wife spoke more than just a few words of English. He had collapsed in a shop and the shopkeeper had summoned an ambulance to take him to the outpatients' department of Park Hospital. Signs and symptoms suggested that he had some abdominal problem, as yet to be properly diagnosed.

He was obviously in great discomfort but resented medication or having antibiotic injections with a view to prepare him for a surgical exploration. He could not make his concerns known or respond to any questions. So he tended to be left alone in his misery.

I felt utterly sorry for him and, although he was not on my side of the ward I answered one of his frantic calls. 'Cornstein sounds like a German name, do you speak German?'

His face lit up and his agitation diminished visibly. '*Sie können mich verstehen*?' (You can understand me?) For the first time I saw a kind of smile on his face. Sister allowed me to spend some time with him to find out something about his situation and health history and to explain why certain tests were done and treatments given. In next to no time at all the cantankerous, wailing bundle of misery turned into a quite amicable and co-operative patient who, while by no means submissive accepted that even painful injections and uncomfortable procedures, like having tubes inserted into his stomach, were not meant to be forms of torture but attempts to prepare him for the operation that seemed to be necessary.

I learned that the Cornsteins had lived in Odessa until recently when their only son, Jascha, had been able to do a deal with the Russian authorities, exchanging several thousand pounds for passports and exit permits so that they could come to live with him in England.

He had come to Manchester to study textile engineering in the late 1930s and remained to finish his studies when the war broke out. He joined the Allied Forces later. His language skills were a particular asset during the end-of-war negotiations in Germany. On return to civilian life, he became a successful businessman in the textile industry.

Jascha and his English wife and son were away on holidays when his father, Mr Cornstein, was taken ill. It had been impossible to contact him in the south of France where they had been touring.

Nobody could have been more relieved than his parents when he returned from his travels. It was interesting to note that Sister and the other ward staff who had so far tried to avoid Mr Cornstein suddenly became very attentive once Jascha, a smart, suntanned man of the world, turned up to see his father. It was the conversation topic of the day when he presented me with a huge box of chocolates and kissed my hand, thanking me for being so kind to his 'Papa'. We were not allowed to accept gifts, however – so the chocolates became ward property.

In a roundabout way the Cornsteins were actually instrumental in meeting my husband later. I became a friend of the family and tried to help the old couple to feel more at ease in England. I knew a Russian-speaking Polish couple who had settled in the area when the Polish army contingent in Italy was dissolved. The Frankowskis were pleased to meet the Cornsteins. Some years later, I met the Frankowskis' cousin in London. He persuaded me to marry him.

Midwifery in London

My three-year nursing course passed fast. I was glad to have had the opportunity to acquire a recognised professional qualification through hard work, which I also enjoyed. Apart from gaining the knowledge and skills associated with various aspects of nursing, I had learned to face traumatic situations, the joys of recovery but also death at times.

I loved the day-to-day contact with patients and their relatives, and the contact with colleagues and superiors in different work settings. Communal living in the Nurses' Home – obligatory for student nurses at the time – provided the basis for social interaction and friendships, which stood the test of time. I am still in contact with some of them fifty years on.

Working long hours but also having regular time off made it possible to enjoy the local facilities like the swimming bath and cinema, which were both close by. Cinemas and theatres in Manchester often sent spare tickets to the Nurses' Home. I remember a hilarious outing to the first showing of *Doctor in the House* in one of the fancy cinemas in Oxford Street, followed by the first Indian meal I ever had in the 'Koh-i-noor' restaurant nearby. We often had parties in our rooms but, of course, outsiders were not permitted on the premises. If anyone dared to have a boyfriend who came to take her out, he would have to wait near the home entrance within the home sister's view. The only available telephone was also there.

I was still in contact with the Bridges, who kept telling me how much they missed me. They certainly missed my work. My replacement from the labour exchange had been totally unacceptable and various temporary help proved unsatisfactory. I often spent my day off in Castleton, doing whatever jobs needed doing for one pound a day. Previously a whole week's work merited no more than two pounds' payment. I got my bus fare as well when no one was available to drive me back to the hospital. These extra earnings came in very useful initially to pay off my debts, then to send off more parcels to my parents who tried to make ends meet in Dresden in the Eastern Bloc after expulsion from our home in Silesia.

Eventually my hard-earned 'riches' provided the means to do a little more travelling, to Scotland and Ireland. In my last training year I even saved up enough to go to Italy. At the time, to get a visa to see my family behind the Iron Curtain was next to impossible.

At the end of our training course, my friend Ann and I decided to do midwifery training in London. We were offered places at the Whittington Hospital in London for the first part of the course, which was hospital-based. We soon got used to a new set of anatomical vocabulary and the intricacies of childbirth. For the second part of the year-long course we moved to Paddington, where district midwifery experience was offered as well as an overview of a different part of the capital.

Ann was attached to a teaching midwife who worked single-handed in Notting Hill, while I joined a group of six midwives working from a Queen's Nurses Home in Maida Vale. The idea was that through working with an experienced practitioner we would learn to use our knowledge and skills in non-clinical settings and gradually take over more and more responsibility for home deliveries, starting with antenatal care and finishing about fourteen days after delivery if no particular problems caused concern.

Miss Harper, the superintendent of the Queen's Nurses Home was a hard taskmaster and expected everyone to act in a disciplined manner. She was a sparrow-like little woman with a big voice and a small appetite for food. She seemed to think that all occupants of the house felt the same way. At mealtimes, minute portions of food were dished up on beautiful plates: no more than two potatoes, a spoonful of the vegetable of the day and the thinnest slivers of meat. We were lucky if we got more than a two-inch square of pie with anaemic custard as a dessert. For breakfast we had lumpy porridge and one slice of toast. Tea was plentiful, but sugar and milk rationed. Ann's midwife was also quite economical. To save on gas she used a double boiler to make the porridge while boiling the egg in the lower bit of the pan. The egg was then taken out and the water used to make the tea.

We were constantly hungry unless we supplemented our diet with goodies from Portobello Road market. Working erratic hours, especially during the night with an empty stomach, was no fun so to keep a private little hoard of biscuits, apples and bananas was almost essential. I don't know why the senior midwives did not complain about the frugal meals – I, as a mere pupil, definitely had no say in the matter.

Next to the kitchen was a large basement room where we sterilised equipment and packed our working bags, always ready for action. When we were on the duty rota we could be called out any time and then would get ready hastily and mount our bikes to ride to wherever someone was in labour. Our district extended from Regent's Park to the borders of Notting Hill, taking in parts of Paddington and Bayswater, including 'Rachman' country, where high rents were charged for very inferior accommodation, often occupied by newcomers to London. The now fashionable area near to the Regent's Canal was a rather grim location in the early 1950s with many sublet houses in various states of dereliction. In one basement flat a rat jumped from the kitchen table when I tried to get some warm water to bathe the newborn baby. In another place vermin had nibbled at the placenta, which, wrapped in newspaper, was waiting to be taken away when mother and baby had been attended to. Few people had washing machines and stacks of spare linen to use, although most of them took care to keep some clean sheets for the delivery and after. Still, Baby S was not the only one to be delivered on a sheet of brown paper with newspaper padding underneath, so the mother would have a clean sheet to lie on after the baby was born.

Of course, some parents went to extraordinary lengths to prepare for the baby's arrival and 'spoiled' the midwife in the process. Many cups of tea and coffee were offered while labour was in progress. Prospective fathers often needed stronger liquids to sustain them through this period. Some of them fainted.

Mr Davies in Sussex Gardens, who was a cook in a local restaurant, insisted on cooking me a full English breakfast at 4 a.m.

in the morning, after his son had been safely delivered. Such breakfasts awaited me every time I called in subsequently on my nursing round, i.e. checking daily for ten days after the birth that mother and baby were clean and comfortable, feeding was well established and no complications gave cause for concern.

Mrs Edwards, wife of the caretaker, chauffeur and handyman in a palatial house in Regent's Park lived in the most elegant environment that I had encountered on my rounds. She even had a bidet in her bathroom, which made attention to hygiene matters so much easier. While I was checking temperatures, blood pressure, milk flow and fundal heights, the umbilical cord and the baby's general condition, the housemaid would arrive with a silver teapot on a silver tray to offer refreshment – crumpets, cakes, etc. I wondered if they knew that the cuisine at the Queens Home left much to be desired.

Another unusual and less salubrious home I was called to was a converted, extended garage, where the baby had arrived before I got there. Two men were fussing around 'Sissy', the new mother, and cooing over the baby, which was wrapped in a bath towel and still attached to the placenta by the umbilical cord. Sissy had had no antenatal care but luckily had a quick and easy labour, which did not harm mother or baby.

I still wonder which of the two attendants was the father – the one with earrings and wearing pink fluffy slippers or the one in the Chinese dressing gown, with plucked eyebrows.

I considered myself very lucky that few emergencies arose during my district experience. We did, of course, try to assure that the pregnancy had progressed normally, that the mother was well and no complications were anticipated, like there might be if the foetus occupied an unusual position in the womb or showed signs of distress. Still, there was always an element of risk: a baby might be born with previously unrecognised defects. (Foetal scanning procedures had yet to be invented and X-rays were rarely done.) Excessive bleeding put mothers at risk when the womb muscles were not efficient enough to expel the placenta and close down the blood vessels to stop blood loss.

This 'uterine inertia' was not uncommon in women who had had several babies in quick succession. I feared that something like that might happen when Mrs Redmond went into labour with her sixth child. She had been advised to have a hospital delivery but refused to go, not wishing to leave 'Charlie' and the kids alone at home.

Miss S, one of the senior midwives, called me at 11.30 one night: 'She has started having some twinges – probably a false alarm. She is not due for a while. Just go and assess the situation and phone in to keep me informed.'

Having assured myself that Miss S would follow the moment I phoned in to report that labour was established, I grabbed my bag and small change for phoning and rushed down Marylebone Road on my bicycle. It proved difficult to find Mrs Redmond's house behind the station by torchlight. The street lamps were all too gloomy or did not work. I noticed that the nearest phone box was at least half a mile away.

When I found number eleven at last, Mrs, Redmond herself opened the door and told me cheerfully: 'My waters have just broken. I should not be long now.' What now? She refused to wake Charlie to run to the phone for me and, seeing the mild panic I was in, she added: 'Don't worry, all my little beggars just slip out without trouble.' And so it happened. I had barely washed my hands and opened my box when she groaned and shouted, 'It's coming.' Redmond baby six cried lustily at 1 a.m. while its father and the other children slept on soundly upstairs. I was relieved to know that 'uterine inertia' was not a problem, especially when the placenta was also expelled intact and the bleeding stopped the moment I had administered the usual dose of ergometrine.

I made mother and baby comfortable, cleaned up the working area and had some tea with Mrs Redmond, leaving her around 4 a.m. in her husband's care. He had got up, because he had to be at work by 5 a.m. at Marylebone Railway Station. 'Nellie from next door will come in later to get the children off to school and keep an eye on the little ones.' I had the feeling that Mrs Redmond's lying-in period was not going to be as restful as it ought to have been.

I need not have worried about not informing Miss S about the events of the night. She had suddenly gone off sick. It transpired later that she was addicted to the potassium bromide and chloral hydrate mixture, a substance we were allowed to give at our discretion to calm mothers down when labour was long and uncomfortable, and painkilling pethidine was not indicated. No wonder that the stock bottle of this rather vile-smelling liquid had often been empty!

Just before Christmas 1955 I became a fully qualified Midwife, having delivered around a hundred babies over the year's course.

Ann also completed her course successfully and, like me, needed a short break before deciding what job to apply for now that we were qualified nurses and midwives. She went to visit her family in Ireland while I spent Christmas in Germany before returning to London, where plenty of work was available, including private nursing, which did not require a long-term commitment.

I found a reasonably priced room in Norfolk Square where Ann joined me later when travelling from Fleet Street, where she had been lodging with relatives, became rather cumbersome. Miss Hill from the Highgate Nursing Agency, who had provided us with odd jobs before, was only too pleased to find more work for us while we considered our long-term future.

London, 1955

Norfolk Square
Nursing at the Masonic Hospital, March 1956

Norfolk Square

1955

Some time ago it must have been grand,
this regency terrace in bedsit land.
Now the stucco is cracked and the pillars peel,
giving the place a rather seedy feel.
The entrance is grimy and the yard a disgrace.
It is not exactly my first choice of place,
but it's affordably cheap that room at the top
and conveniently close to the twenty-seven bus stop.
The room is quite spacious with a small balcony
and rather basic fittings, but that's OK with me:
some curtains, a lamp, some cushions and books
will soon improve its spartan looks.
No en suites here, just a basin and tap
and a bathroom on the landing halfway up.
It does not look all that savoury, this –
it's probably prudent to give it a miss.
Tilly Barcley, the owner, is a fiery redhead.
Somewhat eccentric it must be said;
an aspiring actress with more ambition than flair
who makes grand gestures in to thin air.
She once met 'Larry' and will never forget
her encounter with Gielgud on some stage set.
It did not take long for me to see
the others who shared the house with me.
In the flat below lived Mr Mah and Mr Wong,
two law students who came here from Hong Kong.
They were very polite, carried my case for me,
while Tilly told them not to expect a fee.
The Joneses occupied the first floor suite.
They worked at St Mary's across the street.
Mr Toms was a recluse and rarely went out;

one just heard his budgie as it fluttered about.
Tilly shrugged her shoulders: 'He is a bit bent –
All right with me. He does pay his rent.'
The other back room was occupied
by Mr Brown, who played saxophone every night
in a club in Soho. He was quite a 'dish' –
not exactly my type, but worth a wish.
Miss Masters lived in the basement flat
What she did, one could hazard a guess at that
She had a white poodle and a middle-aged maid
and tended to be out on Pread Street quite late.
When the Joneses moved out I took over their flat.
More rent to pay, but Ann helped with that.
She decided to join me and came to stay,
since her cousins in Fleet Street lived too far away
for our daily jaunts up Harrow Road
where we delivered babies by the load.
At the end of our course we found different jobs
in Hammersmith – with rather bigger nobs.
'They need temps,' said the agency's Mrs Hill,
'I think you will perfectly fit the bill.'
So we rubbed shoulders
with the Knights of the medical zone
at the Masonic Hospital; truly a place of its own.
It had rather a posh and rarefied air:
only masons and dependants were treated there,
unless you had money and plenty of that,
like the plump carpet dealer who flew in from Baghdad.
Ann worked with the children, I was theatre-bound,
where Sir Cecil and Arthur stood their ground
not Tilly's sort of theatre, mind –
more cutting, of the surgical kind.
In off-duty times we enjoyed London life:
cinemas, operas and Mr Brown's Soho dive,
coffee bars on Queensway and Whiteley's store,
Portobello Road market – one could not wish for more.
Then Ann fell in love with Peter Brown
which caused in Fleet Street more than a frown:

A jazz musician, phew! – and almost black!
In the end Ann went off with the more suitable Jack.
Soon after I happened to meet my fate –
at Lafayettes in Regent Street, on a blind date.
He showered me with flowers and chocolates and mail.
But there begins another tale.

Spaghetti Bolognese

Ann's move to Norfolk Square reminded me vividly of my first encounter with her Irish/Italian relatives, who owned a cafe/restaurant in Fleet Street. I suppose you would call it a bistro these days.

I had never heard of spaghetti Bolognese before I came to England. After all, the staple food in our part of East Germany was potatoes. The only type of pasta I knew were home-made flat noodles that floated on Mother's famous chicken broth, along with diced onions, carrots, celery and peas, laced with a sprinkling of chopped parsley. Very good it was.

Once in England I became acquainted with tinned spaghetti, served incongruously on pieces of toast. It did not really appeal to me but I ate it, as well as other unfamiliar foods, like baked beans and tinned tomatoes, which were regular offerings on the breakfast menu at Park Hospital during my nurse training.

It was in Fleet Street that I encountered spaghetti Bolognese first. Alma had invited us for the Italian version of Christmas celebrations. 'You can't spend Christmas Eve alone in that nurses' home,' she had said. So we took the bus to Fleet Street for a most memorable after-midnight party.

We joined the family for Midnight Mass, which was very colourful and melodic. On our return to the cafe and after effusive wishing of Happy Christmas all round, the drinking and eating started, along with music and dancing and general jollifications.

At 3 a.m. three policemen arrived, not in their official capacity but just off duty and as regular customers and friends of the family. After initial toasts on this festive occasion, distributing little presents and nibbling goodies from the buffet table, Brian, a police inspector sighed: 'I am starving – it has been quite a night in the East End. Alma, I could just do with one of your specials.'

Alma, an ever-attentive hostess, did not need to hear this twice and vanished into the kitchen. Less than an hour later she appeared again with a large bowl of steaming spaghetti on a trolley and a cauldron full of Bolognese sauce to go with it. A lump of hard cheese would, when grated, add the finishing touch to the meal.

It was not only Brian who tucked in heartily. Others were lured away from the panettoni and sweetmeats and in next to no time the tasty, sustaining mound of Alma's Special had vanished. Alma had obviously heard all the compliments before but still glowed with pride.

The music, dancing, eating, drinking and joking continued while Ann and I were beginning to get worried about getting back to the hospital in Archway, where we were supposed to be on duty on the maternity ward at 8 a.m.

Needless to say, public transport early on Christmas day was unobtainable and attempts to ring a taxi failed.

Ann's uncle was definitely incapable of driving – he did not even remember where he had parked his car.

So it came to pass that Ann and I were driven back to the hospital in a Black Maria with a rather jovial police escort. Brian justified this unorthodox use of a police vehicle by saying: 'Well, we are supposed to help the public,' adding with a laugh, 'particularly damsels in distress who have babies to deliver on Christmas day.' I don't think the hospital lodge keeper could make any sense of the situation. He even forgot to ask us if we had permits to stay out overnight, when we rushed to get changed for the day shift.

It was not too difficult to persuade Alma to pass her special recipe on to us. It was nowhere near as exotic as I had expected it to be: 'For two to four helpings, all you need is an eight ounce tin of spam or luncheon meat, a tin of chopped tomatoes, some concentrated tomato purée and several cloves of garlic, finely diced. Put all the ingredients into a small pan and simmer gently while the spaghetti is cooking in salted water. In a pressure cooker it only takes ten minutes to cook half a pound of the stuff in about a litre of water. Usually no draining is needed. A teaspoonful of cornflour stirred into evaporated milk and added to the sauce makes it really thick and creamy.'

We did not have a pressure cooker but felt that even we, with minimal cooking facilities (a mini stove with one hotplate and a minute grill-cum-oven), two Woolworth's pans and a Pyrex bowl could emulate Alma's delicacies. In fact, 27 Norfolk Square became quite famous among friends and acquaintances for its so-called Italian cuisine.

The Masonic Hospital Experience

Having had a fair amount of surgical and theatre experience, Miss Hill, from the Highgate Private Nursing Agency, sent me to the Masonic Hospital in Hammersmith where temporary help was urgently needed in the theatre suite. 'They are quite a snobbish lot,' she said, 'but I am sure you will cope.'

I entered the place with some trepidation. The entrance hall was more like the foyer of a smart hotel – all marble chrome and glass with tasteful flower arrangements here and there. However, once I reached the theatre area I was reassured. True, it was spacious, beautifully tiled and laid out, but equipment and procedures did not differ substantially from the ones that I had been used to in my provincial training hospital. Even the renowned specialists who worked here looked quite pedestrian in their loose cotton garments, caps and Wellington boots once they had shed their bespoke suits and bowler hats.

They had their little fads and fancies, as indeed the Park Hospital doctors had done. One liked to work in concentrated silence, which made the hissing of the sterilisers in the adjoining room, the gentle whirring of the ventilators and the rhythmic pumping of the anaesthetic machine more noticeable. It was quite calming actually. There were just some quiet requests for clamps, suction, swabs, catgut, etc. as the operation progressed. Team members such as the anaesthetist and his assistants and the sister in charge of the trolley full of sterile equipment knew exactly what he referred to and what was required.

Another surgeon liked soft background music, Mozart or Debussy, as he worked, while Sir Cecil entertained his team and especially the statuesque senior theatre sister, whom he knew well, with snippets of his public life: 'Had lunch with the "old girl" yesterday,' etc. I was told later that the 'old girl' he referred to was the Queen Mother, who must have been all of fifty-five at the time. He was one of her official medical attendants.

After a few weeks of getting to know staff and routines quite well I was asked if I would consider doing the night shift. Since the hospital had no Accident and Emergency Department, few surgical procedures were carried out at night. The top surgeons did not like to be called out unless a registrar considered that an appendix operation could not wait till the morning, when normal business would be resumed.

Night duty was not popular with the regular staff but I thought I'd give it a go, even though the shift was long – twelve hours – it was a lonely job.

Still, there was plenty to do – mainly getting the theatres ready for the next day's work. After scrutinising the theatre lists of the cases to be dealt with in sequence, I had to choose the appropriate sets of instruments to sterilise and eventually set the trolleys in an aseptic fashion, not touching anything with bare hands. Drums full of sterile swabs and dressings had to be at hand, as well as suction pumps and drip and drainage equipment.

Another of my tasks was to lay out the cotton theatre garments for the surgeons to slip into before they entered their working arena. That meant knowing their preferences and certainly their measurements. Sir A's fifty-inch waist definitely would not have fitted into standard size trousers and vests. He actually liked a blue one-piece, which looked a bit like a boiler suit. I made a list of individual fads to avoid temper tantrums, which had been known to happen when things were not to the gentlemen's liking.

Bandages had to be rolled and metal drums filled with cotton wool swabs, gauze and gamgee pads, ready for steam sterilising if shelves needed restocking.

At midnight I had to go down to the night sister's office to 'hold the fort' while she was having a meal in the rather smart canteen. I always prayed that there would be no awkward phone calls or other tricky situations to be dealt with, and heaved a sigh of relief when she returned, so that I could go for my midnight meal before returning to the lofty height of the theatre suite to continue my routine tasks in a leisurely fashion. Occasionally I heard footsteps down the marble corridor when one of the resident doctors would call to clarify items on the day's work list and stay for a chat. Most of them thought they were very privileged to work in this rarefied atmosphere and tried to impress me with name dropping: 'Sir A promised me some hours in Harley Street', etc.

When my routine tasks were done I was expected to sew nine-inch-square swabs, made of several layers of gauze, folded in such a way that no fraying edges were apparent and sewn with criss-cross stitching to hold them firmly together. I was allowed to use the little electric sewing machine for my own purposes in my free hour. It came in very useful to make the odd cushion cover and eventually even fashion my wedding outfit, which was much admired by everyone who saw it. I surprised myself! I had bought a remnant of brocade at the Jacqumar Sale near Bond Street, which served the purpose admirably. For years the outfit – a scoop neck dress and jacket – hung at the back of my wardrobe until my daughter decided to wear it at her wedding. It fitted her like a glove.

Meanwhile in Manchester

1955

This account of events was put together from eyewitness reports, since I was only at the receiving end of all these efforts.

It was Tadek who suggested that they should bake a special cake for Rosemarie's birthday.

Tadek was married to Vera and Vera was Artur's landlady. Artur had been on a business trip to London where he met Rosemarie, who lived and worked there. Artur was to take a parcel of books for his cousin Edek back to Manchester and pay Rosemarie for them. They had arranged to meet at Lafayettes in Regent Street. Edek had described her as 'smallish, with dark-blonde hair, blue eyes and quite pretty'. When Artur saw her tripping down the road, he fell head over heels in love with her. He had never believed in love at first sight before.

He started to write long letters, speaking of his admiration. She replied politely but made it clear that a closer relationship or marriage were not on her agenda at the time. This was definitely not what Artur wished to hear. He set his mind on winning her over and pursued his goal with fervour in the months to come.

Business trips to London were no longer the chore they used to be. 'I happen to be in London next week,' he would write, 'and have a spare ticket for the ballet in Covent Garden.' To Rosemarie, the opportunity to see Margot Fonteyn dance in Stravinski's *Firebird* was too good to miss. She agreed to meet Artur in Soho for a meal before the performance, and then they had an enjoyable evening at the ballet. She was good company and conversation flowed but definitely avoided references to Artur's previous declarations of affection. He sent her home to Paddington in a taxi and made his way to Euston for the midnight train to Manchester.

More business trips followed and, strangely enough, they tended to coincide with operas or ballets in which Rosemarie had expressed an interest. He always had a spare ticket 'by chance', which he duly offered to her.

When her birthday approached the following year, he suggested that she should come to Manchester for a change, where Joan Sutherland was to take the leading role in *Aida* at that time.

Artur arranged for her to stay with the Tribells. They were an elderly couple who ran a small, ramshackle greengrocery shop where Artur did his weekly shopping. He had endeared himself to Edna, who liked his continental gallantry, and to Frank, who used to be a musician in his younger years and was keen to discuss music and the latest models in gramophones and tape recorders while weighing out potatoes and carrots.

When they heard about Artur's latest attempt to win the young lady's affection, they offered accommodation in their home for the weekend that Artur intended to make a truly memorable event.

In the meantime, Tadek tried to remember the recipe for the Polish nut gateau, a very extravagant concoction he used to create when he was still a baker in Warsaw before the war. It was a 'must-have' for his customers for special occasions. The war had put an end to such luxuries, indeed, to his baking days. He had not stirred or kneaded any dough since he was in a supply team of the Polish troops in Italy in the mid-1940s. The only mixtures he stirred now were abrasive carborundum concoctions in a local factory where good money could be made to keep one's house and family.

Vera tried to discourage him but he was convinced that he could rise to the occasion and bake a masterpiece of a gateau to further his friend's efforts to make Rosemarie's birthday an unforgettable experience.

It was not easy to find the essential ingredients for the cake: walnuts, vanilla pods, rum, brandy or, indeed, large numbers of eggs and plenty of unsalted butter for the cream. Edna came to the rescue and managed to procure the items from a wholesaler she knew, bribing him with some of Frank's treasured cigars.

Soon Vera's kitchen became the setting for serious baking.

Bemused by Tadek's unusual enthusiasm, she left the men to it. Since Tadek could not remember the exact amount of sugar, walnuts and breadcrumbs, nor the correct temperature setting for the gas stove, the first cake base turned out to be a disaster. The mixture rose beautifully, but then collapsed, forming a gluey mass at the base of the tin. Once cold it resembled walnut brittle – quite edible but definitely not what had been intended.

Luckily, Edna's supplies were generous and a second attempt could be made to fashion the cake base. It had to be right this time because no more ingredients were available. Artur stirred the egg yolks and sugar with vigour while Tadek grated the walnuts, diced the vanilla pod into minute pieces and whipped the egg whites into firm peaks, eventually drizzling rum into the finished concoction.

Then they waited with bated breath for the mixture to bake, not daring to open the oven door for half an hour or so and avoiding knocks and noises in the kitchen in case any disturbance of the baking process caused another collapse and disaster.

The cake base turned out perfectly this time: three inches high with a flat, evenly browned top, spongy to the touch.

Vera had to admit that she could not have done any better herself. Edna popped in to admire the result, bringing a small jar of maraschino cherries and a stick of angelica, which could be useful for cake decoration.

Of course, the base had to cool and solidify before further action could be taken. Another six egg yolks had to be procured to lighten the buttercream, which had to be stirred and beaten for what seemed like hours before it was almost white and fluffy.

Vera's bread knife was barely long enough to slice the cake base into three layers, each one to be treated differently. The bottom layer was soaked with red wine before redcurrant jelly was spread on, topped by a layer of coffee-flavoured cream. Brandy was the choice for tier two, plus more jelly and cream. The top tier was infused with strong black coffee and smoothed out with a generous cream layer.

It was quite difficult to even out the sides of the cake. Frank remarked that it was like grouting brittle bricks. Once reasonably smooth, they pressed in grated nuts to give it a sort of rustic finish.

It remained then to decorate the top. Grand designs were suggested: written messages of congratulation, even a musical score – all difficult to achieve in the absence of the elaborate piping equipment Tadek used to have in his bakery. Eventually they piled on the last of the buttercream and made wavy patterns with a fork, scattered chocolate shavings over the top and used Edna's cherries and the angelica to create a bouquet-like adornment in the centre of the cake.

Then they stood back and admired their work of art. It looked good – mouth-watering, in fact.

After all this effort, the precious gateau obviously had to be handled with utmost care while it was taken to the Tribells' house to be stored in the cellar till Sunday.

Frank was beginning to be carried away by the almost childish enthusiasm everyone seemed to display in helping Artur's quest to woo Rosemarie.

'What about some music to wake her up with on her birthday?' he suggested. Artur was only too keen to collaborate in choosing suitable morning music from Frank's classical repertoire.

They withdrew to the front room where the grand piano and most of Frank's music equipment was kept, and started playing, rejecting and choosing suitable melodies for recording. Edna and Vera withdrew to the kitchen while all this editing was going on and had a glass or two of sherry, feeling rather piqued that so much time and attention was lavished on this Rosemarie whom they only knew from hearsay.

Once the music had been chosen it was decided that tunes might be interspersed with verbal messages and a rendering of 'Happy Birthday', sung by Artur, Tadek and Frank, accompanied by the piano. It had to be rehearsed, of course, to ensure that it flowed properly and sounded right. Eventually Frank's latest Grundig reel-to-reel tape recorder was rigged up on the landing outside the room where Rosemarie would be sleeping.

Artur met her at the station when she arrived from London. He took her for coffee at the Kardomah in Market Street, and a little later for dinner in the Cafe Royal – not far from the Opera House, where Joan Sutherland was giving her gala performance in *Aida*. Somehow it did not matter that Aida sang in English while

Radames responded in German. A German singer had been summoned to Manchester at the last moment to replace the male lead who was ill. Anyway, it was a splendid performance and Artur glowed with pleasure, noting how much Rosemarie enjoyed it.

She slept well that night after her exciting, tiring day. When she woke on Sunday morning, sunlight was streaming through the attic window. She was not sure where she was for a moment and thought she was still dreaming.

She heard music – maybe a radio playing? Or a procession in the street below? But no – she could hear it clearly now as the sound of Wagner's *Wakeup chorus* from the Mastersingers increased in volume right outside her door. It was followed by waltz music from the *Rosenkavalier*, a hearty rendering of 'Happy Birthday' and a knock at the door.

Edna came in first to offer congratulations and make sure that she was properly attired in her bedjacket before Artur was allowed to enter, accompanied by more Strauss music, bearing a lovely bouquet of tawny roses. Tadek followed with the gateau on a silver platter and Frank with a bottle of champagne.

She blushed fiercely with embarrassment at being given all that unexpected attention. No one had ever made her feel so special and cosseted.

Artur's persistence paid off. A few months later Rosemarie agreed to marry him.

It is not often that a bridegroom bakes his own wedding cake. Well, Artur did, with Tadek's help, and carried it all the way to London to the reception.

In due course I learned the intricacies of producing 'Torta Orcheowa' myself. It became a must for festive occasions at home and a welcome present for friends, notably the Tribells, Vera and Tadek.

Getting Married

September 1956

Artur was glad when he arrived in London with the wedding cake still intact. He had balanced the hatbox, into which it had been carefully placed, on his knees on the train to London and on the bus from Euston Station to Earl's Court. It would have been a disaster to spoil the contours of the creamy Polish nut gateau, which he had baked himself and had decorated delicately with images of intertwined wedding rings and pink marzipan rosebuds. Roman and Joan, with whom he was staying, were suitably impressed with Artur's work of art. He had been known as a good soup cook sharing a student flat with Roman while studying in London after discharge from the Anders Army in Italy and living on a shoestring.

In the meantime I was frantically doing my part in the wedding preparations. Having no relatives in this country and certainly no parental riches to finance the event, it was going to be a small wedding, very much in a do-it-yourself style.

The Simpsons, caretakers of the house I lived at in Norfolk Square, offered their huge basement living room as a venue for the wedding meal and their kitchen and utensils for me to do the catering.

Whiteley's food hall in Bayswater provided all the ingredients I needed: fake caviar to decorate the canapés that would be offered with pre-dinner drinks, oxtail for the soup and thin slices of veal for wiener schnitzel, to be served with continental potato salad.

I had persuaded a neighbour who had an old-fashioned Daimler to take us to Paddington Registry Office, and a local photographer, whose wife's baby I had delivered during my midwifery training in Paddington, agreed to take some photos at a cut-price rate.

Nobody had thought of flowers, but Ken Wong, a fellow

tenant, came to the rescue by procuring some pink roses and greenery from a shop on Pread Street.

I had barely finished cooking the schnitzel when it was time to get ready for the ceremony at 10.45 a.m. I had made my wedding outfit myself – a rich maroon and gold Jacqumar material, bought at sale time in Bond Street, laboriously stitched into a dress and jacket while I was on night duty at the Masonic Hospital, where I got a two-hour break in a twelve-hour shift. It turned out well and looked good with a toning pink hat.

This was one occasion when Artur could wear his smart navy suit – acquired in Italy after the war in exchange for his cigarette rations. He never smoked. Roman, the best man, looked very smart too and so did Ann, my roommate in her kingfisher-blue dress. They filed into the Daimler with us to be our witnesses.

The short ceremony passed very quickly and in no time we were signing the registers and were on our way back to Norfolk Square. Some of the tenants greeted us there with a bottle of Asti Spumante and the wedding march from *Lohengrin*, played on Ken's radiogram. It was a lovely gesture.

Mrs Simpson had finished setting the table while we were out and had donned a white cap and apron, simulating the uniform of the waitresses at Lyon's Cornerhouse, and Mr Simpson acted ably as the wine waiter. By then, Alan and Molly from Edmonton, whom I had met on holidays in Italy the year before, and Joan, Roman's wife, had arrived to join us for a leisurely wedding meal that was enjoyed by all. There were even some speeches and the opening of telegrams from relatives abroad and cards and presents from friends in the north.

When the last spoonful of trifle, made in Mrs Bridge's style, had been eaten we moved upstairs to the big room, occupied by Ann and me while working in London. We had prepared snacks and drinks of all descriptions to offer our housemates, who also witnessed the cutting of the wedding cake. We laughed, joked and danced, spilling out on to the landing until it was time for Artur and me to trek across London with Roman and Joan to catch a train to the channel ferries and on to Paris.

To go away for a honeymoon was a last-minute decision. By the time we had scraped together a deposit on a house, and with me working extra hours for the agency, we had about a hundred pounds between us. The sensible thing would have been to buy some essential furniture for the house – it was empty apart from orange boxes, two old camp beds and a cocktail cabinet which Artur's colleagues had given us as a wedding present. Still, we decided to take a trip abroad, accepting an invitation from Artur's wartime friends to their family home amongst the vineyards near Bordeaux. Paris was on the way there.

Getting married, Paddington Register Office, 1956

Setting up Home – Return to Reality

It rained and rained. After beautiful September days in Paris, tranquil days with Artur's wartime friends in a little village near Bordeaux and sampling wild grapes on deserted beaches on the Costa Brava, London was a distinctly depressing anticlimax to those heady days. It did not help that our meagre funds were severely depleted after the honeymoon extravaganza, which we had not really been able to afford.

Still, we knew that there would be a roof over our heads when we returned to Manchester. We had managed to put down a deposit for a house and got a mortgage from the Urban Council. However, the prospect of making do with two camp beds and using orange boxes as tables, seating and storage units was not appealing.

On the brighter side, I had already managed to put some home-made curtains up and we had the sliding door cocktail cabinet with a rotating shelf inside, complete with bottles of sherry and port. We also hoped that by the time of our return our gas cooker would have been installed, a top of the range Cannon with automatic ignition, high level grill, etc. We had actually been surprised to see the same model in the window of a Paris showroom, described as the 'Queen of Stoves', and felt proud of our choice. It cost sixty-six pounds – nearly two months' wages – and would take two years to pay off in instalments added to our gas bill.

It was late when we arrived in Manchester, but we managed to catch the last twenty-three bus to our destination.

Artur did not carry me over the threshold since it did not seem wise to put our bags down into the puddles on the steps near the front door. Luckily, the key slid easily into the lock before we entered our home for the first time as a married couple.

Our footsteps echoed in the empty hall, but a surprise awaited us in the small morning room next to the kitchen. While supervising the installation of the gas stove, our friend Edna had made a fire in the 'Cottage Range', which occupied a quarter of the tiny room. Our predecessor claimed that she had done all her cooking, baking and water heating with this contraption. We never found it to be that efficient, but at the time the flames in the open grate gave welcome warmth. Edna had thoughtfully filled a bucket with logs and even provided a brand new poker for our use.

Two old-fashioned easy chairs crowded the rest of the space next to an orange box, which was covered with a tablecloth and topped with a vase of autumnal flowers and a cake with a welcome message. Good old Edna. We were touched by her caring gestures and relaxed for the first time since our arrival.

More surprises awaited us when we explored the rest of the house and realised that we actually had a bed upstairs and would not have to sleep on our primitive camp beds. We heard that Edna's sister and brother-in-law had moved to South Africa but wanted storage space for some of their furniture in case they decided to return to live in England. Why not make use of the stuff?

Edna quite rightly reasoned that storage fees could be saved while doing us a favour. We found that we now had a wardrobe, a chest of drawers and a carpet in the sitting room as well. They would not have been our first choices when buying things, but they served admirably as standbys till we could afford our own furniture. We had enough crockery, pans, sheets and towels from our bedsit days to see us through the first few months as novice householders.

However, mild panic set in when my former flatmate from London announced that she was coming to stay with us over the weekend. We could not possibly let her sleep on the uncomfortable army issue camp bed, so I rushed out and spent a week's wages on a divan and a couple of blankets at Fryers in Eccles.

Ann's visit prompted me to try roasting a chicken, using the baking tray with a spit suspended above it – supplied with our fancy Cannon stove. It was delicious, although I had omitted to take the plastic bag containing the giblets out of the innards.

Ann's visit also gave the impetus for having a house-warming party, for friends we had both known in our Park Hospital days and for those who had been so helpful during Artur's and my courtship.

By then Artur had installed our table lamps and his Grundig record player on yet more orange boxes, of which we had a never-ending supply from Edna's greengrocery shop. Ann's bed had been converted into an oriental divan with bolsters and cushions on a cheap glossy material from the market. The cocktail cabinet took pride of place in the sparsely furnished room and was much admired, as the interior lighting showed up the green, baize-covered carousel now fully stocked with bottles. One or two of them had come from the party guests. Other visitors had kindly brought practical gifts like buckets and plastic bowls with dish mops. One had even thought of a toilet brush in its container, beautifully wrapped and adorned with a big bow made from toilet paper. Well – we had asked for no presents other than little useful items for the household.

Tadek did not go along with this and brought one of his home baked luxury nut gateaux to the party – needless to say, it was appreciated by all. Our first attempt at home entertainment proved to be most enjoyable.

Slowly but surely, our home took shape. I helped an elderly neighbour to decorate a room so that I could learn the intricacies of stripping walls, filing holes with plaster, paper hanging and painting. I became quite good at it, and enjoyed the creative experience while saving the cost of tradesmen's wages.

When Mrs Slynn, the Senior Tutor at Park Hospital, asked me if I was interested in coming to help out in the Nurse Training School, since the other tutor had left, I jumped at the chance. She knew that I had never done any formal teaching but felt I could cope with it. So I started work from nine to five, Monday to Friday, for the princely sum of five pounds per week.

Mrs Slynn taught the more academic subjects like Anatomy and Physiology that had caused me some headaches in the Preliminary Training School (PTS) some years earlier, but I felt reasonably confident in teaching Theory and Practice Of Nursing. This meant planning and making teaching notes, and making conscious efforts to keep the students' attention, which, I soon realised, could not be taken for granted.

The Hygiene Syllabus was also allocated to me. Apart from personal and domestic hygiene it included food hygiene, water supplies and waste water and sewage disposal issues. I don't think modern nurse training entails visits to sewage works and references to 'privy middens' for personal waste disposal. The practice of 'laying dust' on floors with the help of damp tea leaves or sawdust was outdated once vacuum cleaners were introduced, but was still mentioned in the hygiene textbook.

There were test papers from time to time, which made me wonder if my teaching had been as effective as I thought it had been. Some odd facts were stated, but I am absolutely sure that I did not teach that pasteurised milk came from cows that grazed on green pastures and adulterated milk came from cows that had committed adultery.

Since Mrs Slynn knew that I could cook reasonably well, she thought I would be just the person to teach the Invalid Cookery module when it was introduced as part of nurse training. So we made custards, blancmanges, fruit and savoury jellies, beef tea and vegetable and potato soups, which were very popular when we offered them to patients on the wards. One of the assistant matrons had a standing order for our tripe and onion concoction, which I thought might be more flavoursome if the onions had been lightly fried in butter first. It certainly made the rather bland dish more palatable. My students stared aghast when the man from the store delivered whole plaice when steamed fish was on the menu. I was then very grateful for the fish filleting skills I had acquired in Varel.

On the whole, my student groups did well in their final PTS exams and I stayed in the school as an unqualified tutor for eighteen months, at which point a new tutor arrived and I left to have my first baby.

I intended to be a full-time housewife and mother for a while and revelled in domestic bliss – though realising that there was quite a lot of work attached to this and not a great deal of time for leisure and relaxation. Sylvia was a very active baby who caused us many sleepless nights but also gave us a lot of pleasure.

Green Fingers

When spring came, Artur discovered that he rather enjoyed gardening. Outdoor work was also a good antidote to the none-too-healthy air he breathed in daily during working hours in his research laboratory, developing and testing brake linings.

In no time our little garden became a blaze of colour, and parsley, chives and mint grew in profusion. The tiny greenhouse engendered Artur's enduring enthusiasm for growing tomatoes, but he wanted to cultivate other vegetables as well.

When a neighbour mentioned that a plot had become available at Mossfield Allotments, five minutes' walk away from us, he applied for it and got it. Other applicants on the waiting list had rejected it because it was totally neglected and needed hard graft to turn it into a usable plot.

It certainly looked a mess and was totally overgrown. We had difficulties in distinguishing between edible plants and weeds. It was July, so too late for the usual spring planting. That meant that we would have plenty of time to clear the jungle before the next season started.

On closer inspection, we found some luscious strawberries ripening under a thicket of bindweed and noticed a little plantation of raspberries and blackberries at the back of the plot, which promised a reasonable harvest. There was even a stunted apple tree with swelling fruit.

From then on, every free hour, including weekends and holidays, were spent at Mossfield. I joined in when household and childcare duties permitted it.

Almost daily, I pushed the pram to the allotment to dig and weed a row or so to prepare the ground for sowing and planting in the spring.

Sylvia liked her outings and the entertainment that the place provided. When she could sit up, she watched the traffic on Bowfell Road and got excited when planes flew overhead and birds dived into the pond. The other plot holders, mainly elderly men, made a fuss of her and sometimes even invited me for a cup of tea outside the tool shed. Useful advice was given too.

In the first full season we decided to grow simple things like lettuce, peas, beans and cabbages, and were surprised at our success. We had to eat lettuce every day and supplied friends and neighbours with it. I was delighted to find a recipe for lettuce soup, which reduced the vegetable's huge heads into next to nothing in the broth and was surprisingly tasty.

The pea harvest was more manageable and gave the impetus to bottle what we could not eat immediately. Edna gave me my first few Kilner jars. More gifts of the same followed from people who no longer did any home preserving. All I needed to do was find new rubber seals and read up about methods of preserving peas and beans.

Five rows of plants produced over a hundredweight of beans that year. We had enough cabbage to feed an army. I tried my hand at making sauerkraut, but put too much salt in it. There is a saying in Germany: '*Der dümmste Bauer hat die grössten Kartoffeln*' – the daftest farmer gets the biggest potatoes. We certainly had little idea of horticulture, yet achieved this astonishing harvest.

Of course we learned from our early experiences and, over the years, Artur refined his horticultural ambitions. The staple vegetables were still grown, though in more reasonable proportions, but rarer crops became firm favourites, like asparagus and mangetout. Kohlrabi won a novelty prize at a local show, as did giant pumpkins, naturally grown, not force-fed to increase their weight. My flower arrangements, using curly kale, beetroot tops and pink young rhubarb stems with shiny leaves just unfolding, won accolades too.

I got plenty of practice making jellies, jams, chutneys, cordials and wines and became a quite successful competitor at the Urmston Show.

Artur continued trying out new crops – celeriac, artichokes, Chinese gooseberries, etc. He even produced a cross-bred strawberry, which he christened 'Madame Rosemarie' since it had certain curvaceous attributes. It raised many a laugh and was quite palatable too.

In order to cope with the production of ever more tomato juice and purée, we bought an old-fashioned German Alexanderwerk juice extractor that I still use now, nearly fifty years after its acquisition, since I was bitten by the tomato-growing bug like my husband. He grew countless different varieties over the years. His former works manager, with whom he travelled to Australia on business, often told the story from these days. While he was looking for opals, Artur had nothing but seeds for new tomato varieties in mind.

Growing trees from seeds became another passion. We gave dozens of coniferous plants away when they were fashionable, about thirty years ago and one or two originals are still on site. One particularly slim specimen with attractive feathery foliage looked quite beautiful from our lounge window and usefully screened off sheds and fences. Still, we had to fell it when the top branches began to dislodge the gutter and to lift the roof tiles.

Another unwise experiment had been growing a Canadian redwood tree. Who would have thought that the tiny seed which at first grew into a pretty little Christmas tree would shoot to the height of our old lime trees within a few years, spreading its branches in all directions and threatening to engulf Mr Rook's, our neighbour's, greenhouse. Obviously not suitable for an ordinary suburban garden, it had to go. It took three of us a whole weekend to chop off branches, gradually downsizing the stem and eventually digging up the widespread roots. Mr Rook's fence fell down in the process.

Having had its roots constricted in a pot to start with, our ginkgo tree is still growing at a more sedate rate, steadily and harmlessly, which can't be said for the oak tree in the front garden, grown from an acorn found in Germany to justify the original house name 'Oakhurst'. The roots are now obviously damaging the tarmac drive and a true 'oak hurst' would grow if we did not dig the plantlets out where the squirrels had sown the acorns they had harvested in autumn.

I have a suspicion that the house-high larch tree in the back garden is not only damaging our lawnmower with its strong superficial roots which lift the grass sods, but has also sapped the strength of our espalier apple cordons. They look punier each year and produce fewer and fewer apples. The neighbours have not yet complained about it, but then their garden is a jungle anyway.

My indoor gardening was done on a more modest scale. Edna's spider plant and ivy cuttings grew easily enough, tolerating a modicum of neglect, as indeed did the yuccas, indoor palms and aspidistras, which I acquired later. However, flowering pot plants that I was given from time to time tended to die on me.

Still, I do well enough with my historic pelargoniums. Mother had always loved this deep pink, full-bloomed variety, which used to adorn our kitchen windowsills in Kerzdorf.

When my parents were eventually evicted from home by the Polish authorities in 1947, Mother took some cuttings along in her meagre luggage allowance as a living reminder of her roots in an alien world.

They were living in Dresden when I saw them again eventually, and the pelargoniums from Kerzdorf were thriving. I could not resist taking some cuttings back to England with me. They soon began to produce their lovely pink flowers. Taking annual cuttings has kept the species alive and prolific for more years now than I care to remember. They still represent a little bit of home and are very dear to me – even more so than my exotic moonflowers.

Amazon Moonflowers

Until I saw an article in the *Sunday Times* I had not realised what an exotic plant stood on my windowsill. The cactus was actually quite insignificant for most of the time. Vera gave me a cutting and it had grown very slowly for many years. Flat spiky branches splayed out inelegantly and occasionally a triangular or square outgrowth emerged from a spindly base. It was by no means a beautiful plant. On more than one occasion I toyed with the idea of throwing it out or least relegating it to a corner of the green-house. But Vera had died by then and I felt that I owed it to her memory to keep her gift alive and let it vegetate near the kitchen window, thriving despite a measure of neglect.

Then, one year in June, what looked like a stalk with a bud emerged from the knobbly base of the plant. It grew fast, reaching a length of four inches within days, arousing our curiosity.

On midsummer night we came home late after an evening out and were greeted by the most exotic scent. The perfume grew stronger when we opened the kitchen door – in fact, it was almost overpowering. The most unusual flower we had ever seen had opened and dwarfed the plant from which it had arisen. By midnight the blossom had opened to its full splendour, measuring seven and a half inches across. It had brown spiky outer petals, a second layer of honey-coloured ones and an inner double layer of creamy petals, surrounding the yellow centre with a waterfall of stamens. We had never seen anything like this before and stared in wonder.

By morning, the splendour had already begun to fade: the petals started to droop and wilt, the scent subsided. After forty-eight hours the plant was back to its insignificant self again, a state, which was to last till June, came around again the year after. This time, two blossom stems started to grow from the knobbly base. One shrivelled in the early stages of growth, but the other produced a magnificent flower again, more or less on the same day in June. We were better prepared this time and managed to capture the splendour with a camera.

Gardening books and knowledgeable friends, neighbours and folks at the garden centre, were consulted but no one seemed to be able to identify the plant (other than to say that it was some sort of cactus, which we knew already).

Then the *Sunday Times* article appeared. Ralph Steadman, the journalist and cartoonist, wrote about his love of gardening and his unusual way of stimulating growth through playing music, singing or shouting to his plants. He also wrote of his fascination with unusual things, including his Amazon Moonflower. His sketch looked remarkably like our blossom, which prompted me to write to him, sending a photo of our amazing specimen.

Almost by return post came his confirmation: we were owners of and fascinated by the species known as *Selenicerus Grandiflora* also colloquially known as the 'Queen of the Night' or simply the Amazon Moonflower.

The picture he sent showed that his bloom could have been a twin of ours. Enclosed with the letter was also an article by a botanist who had gone to the Amazon rainforests in search of unusual botanical specimens and in her search came across the 'Queen of the Night'.

Ralph became so enamoured with his possession that he wrote and composed an oratorio in celebration of its purity, bemoaning at the same time man's increasing destruction of natural habitats.

When the cactus flowered the year after we made an occasion of the event and played the oratorio, 'The Plague and the Moonflower', while revelling in sight and scent experiences.

When I sent Ralph a photo of that year's blossom he wrote back to say that unfortunately no amount of music, talking and shouting had induced his plant to its usual gala performance. However, his tomatoes were doing extremely well. In response to some of his writings I had sent him samples of my tomato seeds, saying that they always grew well even without aural stimulation.

I took some cuttings from my 'mother plant' some years ago. They produced flowers for the first time last June and seem to be doing well again this year, although for eleven months of the year the cactus is by no means a thing of beauty.

I would love to drift down the Amazon like Margaret Mee, scanning the swampy jungle, and eventually being led to the moonflower by its evocative scent. Wishful thinking.

Treasure Hunts

Our house was gradually becoming a home of our own making. Essential pieces of furniture and carpets were acquired at sales when finances permitted. My growing collection of indoor plants, flowers and foliage from the garden added touches of colour throughout the house all year.

My flower arrangements, using home-grown materials, including beetroot tops, curly kale and young rhubarb stalks with shiny pink leaves just unfurling, gave new ideas to other members of my flower arrangement class, some of whom spent a lot of money at the florist or at the accessory table, where exotic dried sprays and blossoms could be bought.

However, I soon realised that my jam jars and two straight glass vases, which we had inherited from the previous occupants of the house, were not the most desirable containers for floral displays.

My classmates not only had vases of unusual shapes and colours, but beautiful old pottery jugs and bowls, tankards and candelabra, as well as figurines, exotic shells, stones and driftwood, which could add style and shape to their artistic efforts.

Having no heirlooms to fall back on and limited funds to acquire appealing new containers, I heard that jumble sales and junk shops were good sources of unusual items of use, costing pennies rather than pounds.

I had seen notices for local jumble sales in the *Gazette* and on notice boards and decided to see for myself what went on at these.

One Saturday I joined the long queue at the Congregational Church Hall and surged through the door with the others, clutching the two pence entry fee in my hand.

All I could see at first were dozens of trestle tables, piled high with second-hand clothing. Once I had become accustomed to the spectacle, I noticed other items, under or on top of tables, or suspended on hooks – shoes, bags, suitcases, hats and lamp shades, even the odd lawnmower, stacked against the walls next to ironing boards and rolls of wallpaper. One table attracted crowds of people. When I got near it eventually I saw that it was full of the most amazing junk with some unusual pieces amongst it – bric-a-brac at its best. Sales fever gripped me and at the end of the afternoon, two shillings poorer, I emerged from the throng almost unable to carry my treasures: a blue glass vase, a yellow glazed baking bowl that I still use now, an ornate teapot, slightly chipped, which I found out later was a quite desirable Doulton piece. A quaint looking little drinking glass, acquired for three pence, still takes pride of place in my antique glass cabinet. It is about 250 years old and still in a perfect state. I am still very fond of an amber necklace, which cost thirty pence.

Not long after this, I noticed an auction in progress on my way to the market. At the time it was safe enough to leave a pram outside of premises, so I carried Sylvia, then about one year old, down the steps into the bargain basement, where auctions of household items took place from time to time. There was a furniture sale in progress that day, and trade was brisk.

Sylvia enjoyed the novelty of the outing and babbled and waved her hands about when the jovial auctioneer asked with a grin: 'Are you bidding, little lady?' which caused general laughter. I felt quite embarrassed and turned to leave when a pine chest came up for sale.

'Who will give me five pounds for this solid piece with an inside compartment and bun feet?' No response. 'One pound then… thirty shillings.' No one wanted to pay two pounds, which I thought was an absolute bargain. Recklessly I put my hand up and the chest was mine.

I just about managed to scrape the two pounds together and paid the auctioneer when he asked: 'How are you going to get it home? On the pram?' I had not thought of ways to transport it to its destination and had to withdraw thirty shillings from my post office savings to pay a man to do the job. The chest replaced a couple of orange boxes and was most useful as a storage unit for bedding and linen and also as a kind of sideboard, good for displaying some of my newly found jumble sale/junk shop treasures.

At another auction I bought my first picture, a pretty country scene watercolour in a gilt frame for seven and six. Very reasonable though these purchases might have been, my husband was getting rather worried about my obsession with bargains, which despite their good value nevertheless made holes in my housekeeping money.

However, he was placated soon after when I managed to turn a four pound and ten shilling bargain into a fifteen-pound profit. A large water colour 'The Prospect of Whitby' looked splendid in the sales room, but with its rustic frame totally out of place on the wall for which intended.

As chance would have it I saw an advert in the 'wanted to buy' column in the *Manchester Evening News*, indicating that someone was looking for a picture of Whitby as a Christmas present. So just a few weeks after its acquisition the 'Prospect of Whitby' changed hands, giving our Christmas funds a welcome boost.

Looking for and finding old and interesting bits of glass, pottery, pictures, etc. encouraged me to learn more about the world of antiques and arts and crafts items. It certainly enriched my life and still does.

Whenever my busy home and professional life permitted, I went to evening classes or even study weekends to learn more about subjects of particular interest and picture and porcelain restoration. As a long-term member of antique collectors clubs, I have spent many hours in congenial company and never cease to be amazed about the range of collecting fields and the enthusiasm some people display in the pursuit of coveted items.

More Trains and Travel

1959, Dresden

Since our rather extravagant honeymoon, travelling for pleasure had not been on the agenda for us, but when Sylvia was about fifteen months old we decided to try to visit my parents in Dresden to introduce them to their first grandchild and, of course, to Artur whom they knew only from hearsay.

East Germany had by then become the Deutsche Demokratische Republik – the DDR. Given that there was still no official representative of the DDR in London, we inquired directly in Berlin about the steps we had to take to make our journey – months in advance.

Eventually we received a wad of forms to be filled in and realised that, while my German passport would be acceptable to travel with, Artur's 'Stateless Travel Document' was not. Sylvia could not travel included on my passport since she was born in England and therefore a British citizen, requiring British papers. She looked rather cute on her passport photo with her baby face and wispy blond curls.

I think Artur was quite glad that he got a negative reply. He was not particularly keen to enter the Communist Bloc, feeling he might be seen as a traitor since he spent the last war years with the Polish battalion under General Anders in Italy and had opted not to return to Poland after the war. He had even been advised to change his name at the time, since he had been involved in intelligence work. Still, he did not object to me taking Sylvia abroad.

So we applied for entrance and exit visas and a transit visa through Holland and West Germany, filling in very detailed forms. I had to undertake not to demand any help or sustenance from the DDR authorities, not to import foreign currency or more than a prescribed number of gifts for our relatives. We were expected to behave responsibly and to report to the Dresden Police Headquarters as soon as possible after our arrival. I felt as if 'big brother' would be watching us all the way. Still, after all these preliminaries and paying considerable fees, I felt I could not opt out at this stage.

In mid-June I set off with Sylvia, a rucksack, a folding trolley and, of course, our indispensable papers via Harwich and Hook of Holland to West Germany, from where the *Interzonenzug* took us at a prescribed crossing point into the DDR.

Luckily Sylvia took to travel like a duck to water. She slept soundly on the ferry – though she rarely slept a night through at home. She loved the 'tains' – trains, of course. When she was not eating, sleeping, playing with her building blocks or listening for the hundredth time to 'the seven little goats' story, she was entertaining our fellow travellers with her gibberish and imitating the huffing and puffing of the 'tains' and the ship's siren.

We got preferential treatment at the Dresden police reporting office when I produced Sylvia's British passport. The stern-looking official did not even bat an eyelid and even smiled indulgently when, in wandering around the office, Sylvia pulled a drawer out of a cabinet, scattering documents of some sort all over the floor, apparently very pleased with her achievement and beaming at the police personnel.

Oma and Opa, my parents, were of course delighted to see me again and to meet their first grandchild. Sylvia loved Opa's little garden with a cherry tree and managed to drip cherry juice all over her outfit. This did not present any problems since she was dressed in home-made industrial nylon dungarees, which were very easy to wash. I should have patented the garment at the time! They went very well with Ladybird t-shirts. She also had a pretty blue and white dress which her godmother had sent from Canada for going out, but her everyday outfit was much more sensible for travel and play times.

Oma liked to show off her granddaughter in the shop and Sylvia enjoyed the attention she received, as well as the interesting things she could see beyond the large shop window. Russian soldiers from the garrison nearby rode past on their horses or pulled farm wagons with equipment about. 'Big doddies,' Sylvia shouted with glee. She had not seen live horses before but recognised dogs who had four legs, a tail and a shape not unlike that of horses, only smaller in size. We thought she was quite intelligent to make such remarks.

My parents were very sad when the day of our departure came, and made me promise to come soon again, preferably bringing Artur with me. I was very worried about my parents. Mother was clearly not at all well but would not admit how difficult she found it to cope with shop and household. The asthma attacks that had started at the end of the war had not abated and were now affecting her circulatory system.

Sylvia beamed and jumped for joy when she saw Daddy again, who had been patiently waiting for the boat train from Harwich, which was an hour late, while the garden blooms in his hand wilted. 'Thank God you are back,' he said with a sigh of relief. After all, one did hear of people getting lost beyond the Eastern Bloc borders!

Artur had coped quite well in our absence, but slid into a flat spin because the peas had matured quickly and had needed picking, and the raspberries ripened unusually early and would have spoiled if they had not been used in some way without freezers being available. 'It took me ages to bottle the peas – I did not realise it was so complicated,' he said. Six Kilner jars were lined up on the kitchen table for my inspection. He was less successful with his attempts to make raspberry jam. We could still smell the incinerated fruit pulp and the burnt-out pan when we entered the house. Still, there were more berries to be picked.

Sylvia showed Daddy excitedly the 'big doddies' and the 'tains' in the picture book that Oma had given her. She had loved to ride on the *Strassenbahn*, the trams, in Dresden.

Health Visiting

Having a baby brought me in contact with health visitors and the local clinics that offered a range of health related services to the population.

I had enjoyed the personal contact with patients in their own home during my midwifery days in London and felt that health visiting might be interesting when returning to work. I held the required qualifications for health visitor training. The job also had the advantage of more predictable working hours than either nursing or midwifery had and therefore was more compatible with family life and childcare responsibilities.

When I saw an advert in the *Manchester Evening News*, stating that the Salford Health Department was looking for HV trainees to expand their service, I applied. After a somewhat gruelling interview I was accepted on the year-long training course, starting at Manchester Technical College in September 1959. I was going to get a training allowance and my course fee paid, but had to agree to work in Salford for at least eighteen months after completion of the course.

I was able to secure a suitable day nursery place for Sylvia and the promise of Artur's cousin to 'stand in' during an emergency should it be necessary, and embarked on a new career path.

The course entailed attending the Technical College for the theory part of the syllabus interspersed with practical work weeks in Salford with a Fieldwork Instructor as mentor. I soon settled into a new pattern of work and home life. Going 'back to school' was quite enjoyable and certainly enlightening. It was taxing as well since a great deal of reading was required to be able to complete essays and projects, some of them rather dry, like public health laws and statistics.

During practical work weeks, we had to wear a kind of uniform – navy blue items and hats of our own choice – sober, of course. Lisa's, a fellow student's, cute little hat with a tiny veil was definitely not acceptable to the HV Superintendent, although her clients quite liked it.

Our course-related 'observation visits' included Fever Hospitals and Common Lodging Houses but also more pleasant locations like the Cow and Gate factory, where baby milk powders were produced. The managers treated us to a splendid lunch at Churches Mansions; I don't think it swayed me to recommend Cow and Gate products indiscriminately.

After written as well as oral exams, and scrutiny of our coursework, including 'Family Studies', i.e. records of several months of contact with allocated families, we were declared fit to manage our caseload in a given district.

Narrow stairs led up to the office from where Miss Langton, the superintendent, ruled the roost. Her deputy, Miss Warren, had to pour oil on troubled waters occasionally to keep the peace and ensure that Miss Langton's insistence on correct procedure in all circumstances did not cause undue stress or drive the work-force away.

Miss Langton was an ardent admirer of Dr Burns, the Medical Officer, who had a reputation for being dynamic and innovative in the Public Health Services and who could definitely inspire enthusiasm.

He wrote articles and books, gave lectures and was the kingpin of several Health Service Committees. He reminded us that we had a proud tradition to uphold since it was Salford where the seeds of the health visiting services were sown in 1862.

Then a group of well-to-do local women decided that something ought to be done to improve the living standards of families in the slum areas of the town, where ill health was rife and the infant mortality rate extremely high. One hundred years had elapsed since the first 'Sanitary Ladies' began to offer advice on home management and childcare, and avidly distributed carbolic powder and educative pamphlets, which many people would be unable to read. A Centenary Exhibition to commemorate these beginnings was held at the local art gallery in 1962.

Having made my uniform coat myself, it was known that I could use a sewing machine. I was persuaded to make Florence Nightingale's dress for the tableau depicting advocates and pioneers of health education. I had to borrow a dummy from the Co-op store, and with a shawl and a bonnet on her head she looked quite convincing.

My creation was in good company. Harold Riley, the Salford artist, had agreed to paint a series of scenes depicting the grim environment and poverty that prevailed in Salford in the second part of the previous century. I was tempted to buy one of his industrial landscapes and wish I had done so. It would have been a good investment.

There is no doubt that life was tough then for most of the working class population and increased attention to public health issues had improved the situation considerably since then. Still, I was more than surprised to note that many families in 1959 still lived in back-to-back houses with outside toilets and no bathrooms. Old tin baths were still in use and most women coped surprisingly well with the help of the public wash house, where the family wash could be done cheaply once you had wheeled your linen there in a pram. There were no launderettes then.

Once I had completed my year-long training course at Manchester Technical College I was allocated my patch, a densely populated area near Salford Docks. My work was mainly concerned with families who had preschool children – about four hundred and fifty of them.

I received about one hundred birth notifications per annum and was obliged to follow them up as soon as the midwife ceased to call.

New mothers knew that someone from the health department would call and usually made me very welcome, being only too keen to have their new baby admired or to discuss feeding and general coping problems. They found it difficult sometimes to decide whose advice to take, since conflicting opinions might be given by grandmothers, mothers-in-law or well-meaning neighbours in a highly peopled area of terraced housing where everyone knew everyone else's business.

Weekly follow-up visits were advocated by Miss Langton, unless mothers had the time and energy to come to the baby clinic on a regular basis for weight and health checks and any help and advice they might require.

When babies were two months old the immunisation programme started. Not all parents wanted to have needles stuck into their precious offspring, but usually relented when the pros and cons of these preventative measures had been explained to them. Dr Burns was very keen to raise the immunisation rates and believed that his health visitors, who after all were trained nurses too, were quite capable of doing immunisations at home if mothers were reluctant to attend clinics or for those who found it difficult to drag toddlers as well as babies along to the immunisation sessions.

As time went by I got to know the families I dealt with quite well. Some coped extremely well with self-care and the demands of the rest of the family often in trying circumstances. Others needed extra support and help in periods of stress caused by feeding and weaning problems, three month colic, thrush and nappy rashes, or the more difficult issues concerning feckless husbands, interfering mothers-in-law, sibling rivalries and temper tantrums. Some people needed to be reassured first that I had not come to pick faults or to inspect their sanitary arrangements and the cleanliness of their bedlinen, which the early 'Sanitary Ladies' used to do.

Apart from home visiting I held regular clinic sessions and was a school nurse as well. Regular hygiene inspections had to be conducted in the schools on my patch.

It was a novelty to be called the 'Nit Nurse'. There seemed to be a hard core of families whose children were perpetually infested with lice, in spite of gallons of Sassafras lotion and toothcombs being issued to combat the problem.

'Rapid Surveys' of lined-up schoolchildren often picked out defects, like faulty vision, skin and posture problems, and occasionally malnutrition, which required further investigations by the school doctor or in one of the special clinics available in Salford.

Dr Burns decided that health education programmes should be initiated in secondary schools, with the content of the sessions to be decided by individual HVs in consultation with the headmaster or headmistress. Mother Victorine at St Joseph's was quite sceptical at first but agreed to let me do a series of talks on childcare, knowing from experience that many of her pupils would become mothers while still in their teens. However, I had to have my teaching notes vetted to ensure that any references to sex were omitted. Little did she know that I did not need to initiate sex education. In the course of the sessions my fourteen-year-old class members asked enough sex-related questions to cause me serious embarrassment – in fact, I was lost for words at times but promised to find answers to their queries if I could, to clarify the issues and dispel some myths. The childcare sessions were voted to be a great success and were followed up with series on Home Nursing and First Aid for which little certificates were available from the Red Cross when certain tests had been completed. For some of the girls, these were the only certificates they ever gained.

Occasionally we had to drop all routine work to be available for one of Dr Burns' special campaigns, like the time when two cases of paralytic poliomyelitis were diagnosed in Manchester. The whole of the as yet not immunised population of Salford, irrespective of age, were offered instant vaccination. People actually queued around the block in which the clinic was situated and we could not boil up the required syringes quickly enough without causing delays. At that time oral polio vaccine was still in its trial stages. After two days, the vaccine had run out. No cases of the infection were notified in Salford. If our efforts had anything to do with this we of course never knew, since it is always difficult to ascertain what has been prevented from happening.

'Don't you miss the more dramatic side of hospital work?' someone asked me once, 'you know – people being admitted who are at death's door, having operations or fancy treatments, and then walking out again smiling after a while?'

Health visiting was certainly different, but no less demanding or interesting once I had realised that there rarely were quick-fix solutions to problems and that, as a visitor to people's homes, they needed to accept and trust you before taking advice and guidance or being willing to air concerns which were not immediately clear and yet made their life a misery.

Obviously we had to keep records and account for our time on duty. Monthly statistics were presented to Miss Langton, who scrutinised them minutely and made comments when she thought that we had not done enough home visits. It was not always easy to convince her that the quality of visits was often more important than the quantity of contacts.

The immunisation rate in my district actually increased markedly over two years and the infestation rate in schools went down. Occasionally I was heartened by an incident that demonstrated that initially quite resistant mothers were beginning to take some health education advice on board – like Mrs Morris, who after one of our dental health campaigns, went to the chemist to buy a toothbrush. She was reported to have asked for a 'strong one', because 'there were ten of them in the house'. Still, it was a move in the right direction.

Beyond the Berlin Wall

1961

Two years after my trip to Dresden with Sylvia, we decided to take Artur along with us. Stateless travel documents were then acceptable, providing they carried the correct visa.

This time it took only six weeks to receive the important looking documents for all of us from the DDR authorities in Berlin, which would ensure a smooth transit to and from Dresden, via a prescribed border crossing.

What we had not reckoned with was that the chosen travel date, 13 August 1961, was the day when the Iron Curtain came down with a bang and the Berlin Wall was erected – at least, the beginnings of it. We did not know about this until we reached Dresden, but realised that something strange was going on as the journey progressed.

The West German border controls were as smooth as before, but the young customs officer could not help making a comment: 'What a mixture of a family. Well, the best of luck to you in the East.'

The East German officials who had boarded the train at Obisfelde scrutinised our papers minutely and questioned Artur closely about his intentions in Dresden. How did he come to live in England? He replied that this was none of their business.

When the train stopped in Magdeburg we thought it was just for the customs personnel to alight. We were mistaken. Two of them entered our compartment again and demanded that Artur should accompany them. Bemused, I and my fellow travellers watched what was happening on the platform.

A woman commissioner, clad in a black uniform with woollen stockings wrinkled round her lower legs, once again examined Artur's papers closely. She looked a bit like Fräulein Rutsch at home whose forbidding appearance had earned her the nickname *Männerschreck* – man's terror.

213

By then all the passengers craned their necks to watch the spectacle and the train driver became more irate by the minute because of this unscheduled delay, which interfered with his timekeeping, something to be avoided at all costs if he wanted to fulfil his *soll*, i.e. reach his performance targets.

He was told to carry on, to which I objected. I got out of the train with a confused Sylvia in tow, making it clear that we were not going to travel on without Artur. *Männerschreck* was obviously in a quandary as to what to do when I suggested in my best German that, if they had any doubts about Artur's presence in the DDR, to avoid further delays for all, they could arrange for us to be met in Dresden by whatever officials they saw fit to do so, since we would be confined on the train anyway and therefore unable to escape en route. It seemed to make sense to her and the train puffed off speedily. If it had been possible we would gladly have travelled to where we came from. Our fellow western travellers sympathised with us, while the East Germans did not dare to offer an opinion.

We actually did not encounter a reception committee when we reached our destination a few hours later but found Mother and Father in an agitated state. While they had looked forward to seeing us they felt that it was not really safe for us to be there. The radio had blared out the news all day that stricter border controls had come into force – officially to stop undesirable elements entering the DDR, but actually, as it turned out, to halt the ever increasing emigration of East Germans to the West, which was depleting the DDR of academic and skilled personnel at an alarming rate.

There had, of course, been fairly strict border controls ever since the Russian Zone, later renamed DDR, had been established, but in Berlin some loopholes permitted folks to go west via the underground system and airlifts to West Germany. From now on all such gaps would be plugged, a wall built and security measures along the whole length of the DDR border strengthened – with cleared strips of no-man's-land, barbed wire and floodlights on observation towers.

The next morning, at 8 a.m. promptly, we presented ourselves at the Police Headquarters to register our arrival and find out more about our particular situation. Father came with us. He had to wait downstairs while we were ushered to the 'Western Visitors' area. We were treated with the utmost courtesy and no one queried our papers and permits. When I drew their attention to our experiences at Magdeburg, they pretended they had not been informed of this and apologised for the treatment we had received at the hands of 'ignorant' officials. They assured us that no harm would come to us and that we should enjoy our stay in their beautiful town to the full. We were not totally convinced of their sincerity and stayed only for a week rather than the planned fortnight.

We tried to be calm and make the best of the lovely August days with my parents. We took them on a paddle steamer for a trip on the River Elbe. Sylvia loved the funicular railway, which took us to a smart restaurant on the hillside above the river. We came down in the cable car later.

By then some of the famous art treasures which had been acquired by the Saxony rulers, notably August the Strong, had been returned from Russia to Dresden. The works were too well known internationally for the Russians to lay claim to them.

Part of the Zwinger, the Baroque Art Gallery, had been restored and now housed pictures and other objects again. There were Rembrandts, Titians, Dutch Mater paintings and, of course, works by Canaletto and Bellotto, who had loved Dresden and recorded its splendour in their paintings, which later served as blueprints for the restoration of the city after the damage done by the infamous air raids at the end of the war.

Sylvia, then three-and-a-half-years-old, was not as impressed with the works of art as I was. She liked the Raphael Madonna 'with the little angels', but thought that some pictures were rather rude with all their naked ladies. She felt sorry for the people with 'all these hurties' in the sculpture gallery, where ancient Greek statues stood, some of them lacking arms, legs or even heads. She has changed her views about art objects considerably since then.

My parents approved thoroughly of Artur as my husband, being as charming, attentive and devoted to his family as he was. Any misgivings they might have had about his Polish origins were dispelled when they realised that his life had been as erratic and unpredictable as ours – if in a different way.

He was born in Posen when West Prussia was a German province, to a German mother and a Polish father, and had a German birth certificate. When West Prussia became Polish after the First World War, the family became Polish citizens.

At the beginning of the Second World War the population of this region was graded into *Volksgruppen*, according to their background. Artur fell into a category which was not German enough to be eligible to hold a German passport and therefore not fit to become a German soldier, but acceptable to work for the Germans in another capacity. Having studied chemistry and being a fluent German and Polish speaker, he was appointed as area *Milk Kontrolleur*, which included visiting the farmers in his district and checking on purity and composition of the milk and its production. He said he felt totally inadequate to advise on stud policy as he was supposed to do but somehow muddled his way through tricky situations. He did this job for the first war years, apparently to the full satisfaction of the authorities. The farmers he visited went out of their way to be in his good books to get positive reports and often sent him home with bagfuls of peas or some eggs. He rode around on his bike to places in easy reach, carrying his testing equipment and paperwork in a large box near the saddle. To more remote estates he went by train. He was always well fed and accommodated by his landed gentry clients, who also provided horse-drawn wagons to take him to the next appointment. In one of the large estates the lady of the manor tried to persuade him to become her personal secretary and manager while her husband did his duty as a high-ranking officer in the German army. It appears that she was not the only one to fancy an available male in his mid twenties. Artur maintained, however, that it never occurred to him to yield to temptation.

As the war went on and more personnel were needed by the German army, Artur's *Volksliste* rating was upgraded to make him eligible to be drafted into the army.

He went for his initial drill and training to a camp near Meissen in Saxony, at which one of the staff officers thought that because of his university education and language skills – he had a fair command of English and French as well as German and Polish – he might be a good candidate for the secret service. So he was sent to what he called a 'spy school' for some months, until higher authorities decided to stop his further education, maintaining that he was a bad risk in the intelligence services because of his unclear loyalties. As a result he was sent to France to guard a German ammunition dump in the pinewoods near Bordeaux – the most boring occupation he ever had. It was during this time that he established a lifelong friendship with a French family.

When the Americans landed in the south of France Artur, as a German soldier, should have become their prisoner. There was talk about internment in Canada for the duration of the war. However, when the interviewing officer in charge heard about his unusual background, he suggested that Artur might make a useful addition to the Polish army in exile, with its headquarters in the Naples region. He was duly shipped there. It was not his fighting skills that were in demand (he had had no practise anyway), but his linguistic abilities. So he became an interpreter-cum-secretary to General Anders, the Polish army leader, until the war ended.

Like most of his compatriots he decided not to return to the Communist Bloc in Eastern Europe but to try to establish a new existence in the West. At the expense of the exiled Polish government he studied for a while in Rome before completing his chemistry degree in London and beginning to specialise in friction materials in the clutch and brake lining industry in England.

While in Dresden we had expected to meet Karlheinz, my younger brother, but his leave was cancelled because of the precarious political situation. He had grown up in Dresden. After doing his National Service, he remained in the navy in the Baltic Sea as a ships engineer. He was supposed to break any connections with relatives living beyond the Iron Curtain, but refused to do so. This could have got him into trouble had he not been indispensable on his old ship, as he seemed to be the only one who knew how to handle the engines.

I was more worried about my parents than ever when the time for our return journey came – after more encounters with officialdom, of course. Mother's persistent asthma had resulted in more circulatory problems. We left with heavy hearts and never saw her again. She died the same year just before Christmas.

The permit to attend the funeral came too late. I might have found it difficult to travel anyway. I was expecting my son, Roman, by then. Morning sickness on top of flu and the sadness of mother's end made for the most miserable Christmas I ever had. 'Never mind, Mami,' Sylvia said when I burst into tears once again, as the duck Artur had bought for our dinner turned out to be the toughest bird I had ever cooked. 'We could put it in the pressure cooker.' This we did and had a reasonable sort of duck stew for our Christmas dinner.

My father died three years later. I had managed to introduce Roman to his grandfather when he was two years old, after another cumbersome trip to the DDR. He still remembers the tin bath on Opa's balcony, where he could splash about to his heart's content on hot July days.

I still feel an overwhelming sadness about the way my parents' days ended.

Motherhood and Family Life

Everything went well when Sylvia was born. Apart from rather troublesome morning sickness, which seemed to last all day for months, I was well and said to be 'blooming', although I was considered to be an 'elderly primipara' since I was thirty at the time. When labour started, progress was rapid. The midwives in the maternity ward would not believe this when I told them so. 'It will be some time before you are fully dilated,' they said and gave me another dose of pethidine to dull the pain and placate me. People like me who had nursing and midwifery knowledge were thought to be overanxious and overreacting in these circumstances.

When I had walked up and down the corridor and been to the loo several times in the next half hour, I knocked at the office door where the night staff were drinking tea and demanded some attention. 'Go back to bed,' I was told, 'we will examine you in a minute.'

'My god – get the delivery room ready,' shouted Sister S a little later, when she had tried to perform an internal examination and was showered with amniotic fluid as the membranes containing the baby burst.

In no time I was wheeled into the delivery room on a trolley. Our daughter was born just ten minutes later. Fortunately the late administration of pethidine had not affected her as it might have done. She broke into a lusty cry immediately. She arrived on 19 March, the exact EDD – 'expected date of delivery'.

There seemed no reason why I should not have a home delivery for my second baby, four years later. My doctor was all in favour of it and after the usual blood and urine tests, physical examination and blood pressure checks, I was given the address of the local midwife and booked her, as well as a home help.

I continued to work as a health visitor in Salford and all went well, apart from a few trying weeks during early pregnancy.

The midwife came to see me from time to time, to make sure

that the baby was growing as expected in relation to the EDD and that it was in the right position for its entry to the world. Ultrasound scans had yet to be invented. She checked the heartbeat with an old-fashioned but perfectly functional ear trumpet.

The list of requirements for a home delivery included not only the things one would expect, like changes of bedlinen, baby clothes and nappies, but also piles of newspaper and brown paper – to protect bed and flooring. I never found out why the jug I had to provide had to be made of pottery with a minimum capacity of two pints. It took me a while to locate one in a little hardware shop in Salford.

July came, with very hot weather that made me gasp for breath at times in my bulky condition. I had stopped working by then and was cleaning the house from top to bottom so that neither midwife nor home help had anything to complain about. All was as dust-free and wholesome as possible, except for the kitchen.

'You promised to do the kitchen ceiling,' I reminded my husband for the umpteenth time. It did look a mess after the leaking roof had been repaired. The expensive water-resistant, steam proof wall and ceiling covering had already been cut to the right lengths and widths. They just needed gluing to the kitchen walls and the ceiling, which was not particularly large nor very high.

'It will be done before the baby is due,' Artur said. 'It should be a doddle.' Eventually he got the ladder in and a thick board to rest on the ladder and windowsill, to make a sort of walkway. 'It won't take long to do it,' he said as he wielded brushes and glue bucket importantly. I hovered about with a long broom in my hand to hold the paper in place where he had first attached it so that he could unfold and glue on the whole length across the ceiling. The first length went on without any problems. It really looked good. The second strip was more difficult to apply since it needed to be properly aligned with the first one, but we managed to do so. However, the third piece yielded to gravity. I managed to support it on one side with my broom for a while, but the middle bit just would not stick. It detached itself from the ceiling before Artur had time to flatten it out with his wide brush against the plaster. It dropped off and hung in a sticky mess, draped over Artur's head as he stood on the ladder swearing under his breath. What now?

I decided that the only way to salvage the situation would be to climb on the gas stove to lift one end of the paper off Artur's head and reattach it to one end of the ceiling, holding it firmly so that he could manoeuvre the rest into place.

I suppose it was not really such a good idea to engage in that form of exercise in my advanced state of pregnancy. Still, it saved the day and I felt triumphant when I saw Artur disentangle the mess and eventually achieve a nicely finished surface. I was waiting to be helped off my high perch when my 'waters' broke and the gas stove was showered with amniotic fluid.

There was no pain, no obvious discomfort other than soaked underwear. In fact, I instantly felt pounds lighter and found breathing much easier.

I phoned the midwife, who advised me to rest and wait for labour to start. Alas, nothing happened – the womb obviously was not programmed for contractions just yet. I actually slept better than I had done for a while.

'We will give it a day or so before doing anything else.' Midwife and doctor agreed on that, but I knew as well as they did that it was potentially dangerous for the baby if this state of inertia persisted.

'You will need to go to the hospital to be induced,' I was told a day later. Reluctantly, but accepting the necessity, I walked to Park Hospital, accompanied by Artur and Sylvia, to allow a pitocin drip to give labour a kick-start. The day after, Roman was born, just a week before he had been due to arrive.

As it was, our frantic efforts to beautify the kitchen had not been necessary. I never got my home help. She had not returned from holidays when we needed her. Still, we coped all right even though Artur could not get time off from work. Paternity leave had yet to be introduced.

Sylvia soon got used to having a baby brother and gave her friends in the day nursery a running commentary on what was going on at home. One day she invited her three little friends from the avenue where we then lived to witness the spectacle of breastfeeding. I was a little embarrassed at first but, noting the girls sitting there awestruck, I realised that it was not such a bad idea thus to introduce these mothers of the future to a perfectly natural function.

Sylvia entered 'proper school' that autumn and Roman occupied her pram as I followed my daily routines, including trips to the market, necessary allotment work and, of course, taking Sylvia to school and taking her home later – generally leading a very contented if unexciting family life.

The year after, Mrs Hohenhaus, a former colleague from Salford, married to a German ex-prisoner of war, asked if I would consider having an au pair girl. Her niece from Hamburg was very keen to come here to learn English. I had never thought of this kind of arrangement but mulled the idea over. Having met the niece and finding her to be a very pleasant young woman, we agreed to take her into our home, as long as I could do at least some part-time work to meet our expenses.

When a health visitor's post came up in nearby Old Trafford, I applied. Dr Sharpe, the Medical Officer at the time, thought it was just up my street, and not just literally. The clinic where I would be based was not too far from home, but I would need a car to be able to cover my district work and do a daily minor ailment clinic at the Open Air School in Longford Park. The latter included some routine clinical treatments like giving injections and offering 'postural drainage' to cystic fibrosis sufferers to clear their airways and make breathing easier.

The idea of having a car appealed to me. It would save me time and make it possible to get home at lunchtime to ensure that 'Sidi', as Roman called our new family member, was coping all right. I need not have worried: Sigrid and Roman fell in love with each other immediately and felt sad when she went home after a year, clutching her English certificate and still revelling in the fact that she had met the Beatles the summer before when they gave a performance at the Urmston Show that made the local girls swoon.

My father had saved Volkswagen stamps before the war to acquire the 'People's Car', promised to all workers in Hitler's time.

Father never got his Beetle since war broke out and all vehicles were required for war efforts, but I decided to have one now. They were of course freely available in England in the sixties, since the Allies saw fit to begin taking up their production again after the war. I had passed the Wolfsburg factory several times when crossing the East German border. It felt strange to be able to acquire a vehicle that Father had coveted so many years ago.

The little blue Beetle was a family favourite for many years to come. Others liked them too and were proud of them. At one time it was the custom to greet other VW drivers in passing with a nod or a wave.

It was twelve years since I had driven the Bridges' Ford, so I took some revision driving lessons to bring me up to date. Still, this did not prevent me knocking the new plastic drawer handles off Artur's workbench when I drove the car into the garage for the first time, and nearly demolishing a drainpipe when I reversed out.

Taking the car out for a spin became a treat at weekends when allotment duties or other urgent work allowed it. We discovered the delights of Smithills Coaching House in Bolton, which could be combined with picking berries on what we called Blueberry Hill. We found mushrooms and wild blackberries in an old quarry near the Redway Tavern and had lunch in a railway carriage near the Little Mill Inn or in a canal boat. Even having tea in one of the newly built motorway cafes had its attractions. The children loved watching the traffic on the M6 from the bridge of Knutsford Service Station.

One day the Beetle got stuck in the sand at Southport Beach. We also realised that we had forgotten to bring matches to light Artur's little spirit stove for his tea brewing ritual, which accompanied each of our picnics. In the end, a group of burly sunbathers helped out with a cigarette lighter. They enjoyed a cup of tea with us before pushing the car on to a firmer surface, ready to go home.

When Miss Garvey, a colleague at the clinic, offered to let us have her weekend cottage in Wales for a beach holiday the year after, we jumped at the chance.

Sigrid had by then been replaced by Annie from Wurzburg, who began to consider us as her second family. There had been a few weeks when glamorous Gaby, the au pair girl from hell, stayed with us. She was a danger to herself and others and would not take any advice. One day, instead of using the boiler intended for the purpose, she used my beloved pressure cooker to boil up her white hankies and pants. She had not thought that putting her foam padded bra and dark tights in as well might spoil the whole lot! I could not help experiencing some Schadenfreude but felt sorry for her as well and gave her some money to replace essential items. Her mother entreated us not to send her back home since she had had 'no end of trouble with Gaby' and just could not cope. Anyway, Gaby found herself another job in a richer household. We felt sorry for that family, but she did not stay there very long either.

The cottage in Wales, 1965

Sand dunes, Wales, 1965

Our first home, Carrsvale Ave, 1966

Result of 'green fingers'
Prize-winning exhibit at the Urmston Show

And Coco Came Too

Gronant, North Wales

It was not a fashionable seaside resort we headed for, nor did we expect to be enveloped in luxury once we got there, but we knew from experience that we would feel at home at the cottage and that our newest family member could be accommodated too.

The car behind us at the Queensferry bypass nearly collided with our own when the distracted passengers tried to make out if the kitten which sat on the shelf behind the back seat of our Beetle, was a real one or one of the nodding-head toys that were popular at the time.

Coco was real enough, a beautifully marked tabby with a haughty little pink nose and huge green eyes, which looked with curiosity into the world that was still strange to her. She was a recent, unplanned acquisition – too young to be sent to a cattery or to be left at home to fend for herself when our holiday week approached. So we decided to take her with us. She was placed into a padded box with air holes and placed on to the back seat with Annie and the children. However, when the fierce scratching from within the cardboard cage became intolerable, we released her – to find that she actually enjoyed the experience of car travel: no creeping under seats or hiding amongst the boxes of provisions which we had been unable to cram on to the car's limited luggage space. Being petted and cuddled soon lost their attractions. She wanted to see what was going on and jumped on to the back shelf, where she remained for the rest of the journey, surveying the landscape through the rear window.

Eventually we turned off the main road on to a sand track, which led to our destination. There were a few proper houses and bungalows in Gronant, but the large expanse of grassland beyond the village, between the North Wales rail-track and the sea and sand dunes, was dotted with a motley collection of prefabs and makeshift huts, albeit set in their own gardens.

Miss Garvey's father had built the cottage when he retired and spent his summers there till he died. Now Miss Garvey let trusted friends use the place while she lived in a gypsy caravan on the adjoining plot.

The place looked quite inviting, with the wooden exterior painted green and a white trellis structure hiding the rainwater butt and the toilet hut. The living area consisted of two fairly large lino covered rooms, one for cooking, washing and storage purposes, and the other as a sitting and dining room, with an ancient leather settee in front of an open fireplace, with logs piled in a corner and a blackened, huge iron kettle on a trivet. Three lean-to sheds had been added to the sides of the main structure, just big enough to hold bunk beds and a double bed that could only be accessed from one side. We did not like to use the primitive earth closet outside at night, so had to make do with an antique floral-decorated toilet bucket near the entrance porch, or even old-fashioned chamber pots. Still – no one seemed to mind this temporary return to the practices of days gone by.

Miss Garvey always made sure that we had enough gas in the cylinders for cooking and lighting purposes. A man with a cart on bicycle wheels came from time to time to deliver propane gas and collect the empties. We did not often light the pendant lamps, which hissed when they were alight. By the time darkness fell we were usually ready for bed. One could always read by candlelight anyway!

Water for drinking and cooking had to be collected from a standpipe a few hundred yards away. We took it in turns to fill buckets or water cans and also made shopping expeditions to the mobile grocer, who brought milk and bread and a few other absolutely essential food items like baked beans to the Warren. His ice cream tubs were a particular favourite.

We all loved the place and the leisurely way of life there. The main attractions were the beach and the sand dunes, a few minutes' walk away from the cottage. Even when the tide came in the water was shallow and it would have been difficult to swim, let alone drown there. This made it an ideal, safe playground for a young family. We tended to rent the cottage at the end of June when few people were around and thus had large expanses of beach to ourselves. The children never seemed to tire of digging canals, building castles and making creative sand pies with all kinds of kitchen equipment. Miss Garvey's colander is still buried somewhere in the dunes.

Even Coco joined in. We had intended to keep her safely locked up in the kitchen with a woolly nest, food and a sandbox, but since she never left our side and followed us wherever we moved, we felt it was safe enough to take her out to play with us. She soon got used to the feel of soft sand beneath her paws and explored the thatches of beach grass, from which she emerged like a little tiger from the jungle. She even followed us wading in the shallow water, not knowing that cats don't really like water. When it reached her belly, she leapt out complaining.

Beachcombing was another fascinating occupation. Shells and stones of various shapes, colours and sizes were collected, sometimes even 'jewels' – bits of coloured glass that had been smoothed and rounded through prolonged contact with sea and sand. There was a little cove where the tide tended to deposit particularly interesting items, like old tyres, driftwood, tins, plastic toys and bottles, which were closely examined in case they contained any messages. We once found a dead sheep and what appeared to be a human arm. It was actually, thankfully a piece from a tailor's dummy.

If we felt energetic enough, we walked as far as the Talacker lighthouse. It looked quite splendid from a distance but was actually out of use and in a sad state of disrepair. Walking in the other direction along the beach we could reach the nearest seaside resort. One of the first places encountered along this way was the gambling den where it was quite easy to lose a week's pocket money on the 'shove the penny' machine. Oh, the excitement of it all. The last time we went there we had to walk all the way back to Gronant along the wet and windy beach because we had no money left to board the bus. We dried ourselves in front of the log fire. Coco curled up on the fender and loved it. We tried to light the old brass and glass oil lamp that evening as a special treat, but obviously did not work the mechanism correctly, since the glass mantle sooted up almost at once. We found it extremely difficult to clean without the proper implements and had to confess our misdeed to Miss Garvey.

This was one of the rare days when rain stopped outside play and we actually made use of the card and board games in the cottage, and played some records on the old wind-up gramophone – quite a novelty. The rain was still pattering down on the corrugated iron roof when we went to bed, but it was bright enough again in the morning to think of further outside pursuits.

The sands were still uncomfortably wet and cold, but there were other things to do, like driving up to the monastery, where the shop sold lovely crunchy biscuits and the honey and jam that Miss Garvey liked. We usually bought her some, taking it with us when she invited us to her caravan for afternoon tea. That in itself was quite an adventure – having tea in a gypsy caravan is not an everyday event. There was barely enough space to seat five of us and, of course, the hostess, who did actually not look unlike a gypsy in her flowered skirt and with a headscarf on to hide her thinning hair. Coco had to stay out for a change in case she got too interested in Miss Garvey's goldfish or the canary whom she shared her summer home with.

Another popular trip was that to the bluebell woods on the hillside beyond the railway line. A tiny little cottage had been converted into a cafe for summer visitors. One could sit in the garden, where numerous ornamental dwarfs and frogs inhabited the rockeries and flowerbeds. The tortoises were real.

It was amazing how quickly and pleasantly the days passed at Gronant, primitive as our abode was and without radios, television sets or computer games. Coco slept all the way home. I suppose we were all in need of some rest after so many active days, but vowed to return again next June, if Miss Garvey would have us.

Years later Annie, who had been our au pair girl at the time, wanted to show her own children where she had spent a couple of unusual holidays with us. Alas, the Gronant Warren had changed beyond recognition. It had become a huge modern caravan park with security guards and leisure facilities. We had managed well without them.

'Beetling' Abroad

Once the children's sand pie days were over and Miss Garvey's cottage was beginning to lose its appeal, we decided to visit some of our relatives in Germany, taking advantage of one of the smart car ferries from Dover which would deposit us and our blue Volkswagen Beetle in Ostend, not too far from our first destination.

Artur had by then got a driving license and was occasionally using the company car to drive to and from work. He did not really like driving and a near miss on the East Lancashire Road, when the handbrake came off as he tried to make an emergency stop, did not increase his enthusiasm or confidence. So I became the family driver.

I had driven for some years by then – in connection with work and social outings – but had never ventured abroad before. By the time we reached the new plantation of tiny fir trees on the hillside near the Keele exit of the M6, I suddenly had what almost amounted to a panic attack. What was I doing – driving my family abroad, miles away from home, not being at all familiar with driving etiquette on the continent nor the roads we had to take to Mönchengladbach that evening? Still, the momentary panic passed and we managed to drive the car without problems to Dover and into the bowels of the ferry on time, and enjoyed the very comfortable crossing to the continent. I would have liked a gin and tonic to steady my nerves, but wisely stuck to coffee.

Gingerly I drove the Beetle on to land and was just about getting used to driving on the wrong side of the road when we reached a small town with rather uneven cobbled streets and no signposts indicating which way we had to turn, and we came to a kind of market square. The local drivers did not appear to adhere to any kind of highway code and just raced across the square with no apparent lane discipline. It took me some time to find the courage to make a left turn in what I hoped would be the right direction for us. One or two drivers had already overtaken me at the corner, cutting across my path and hooting frantically. It was getting dark by then but we saw a sign for Mönchengladbach at last and eventually reached my cousin's home, having taken a few wrong turns in the town itself.

Hanne and her family were quite worried by then. They had expected us hours ago and held up their evening meal for us. We still enjoyed it, however at 11 p.m.

The next lap on our travel itinerary was less hazardous. Well signposted, smooth, quiet country roads took us to Iversheim/Münstereifel in the picturesque Eiffel region, where my aunts had built themselves a little bungalow on the hillside. As displaced persons, they had been offered a piece of land quite cheaply by the local authority, to enable them to create their own living accommodation. Some farmer friends helped them to level part of the hill to build on. To save money they then dug their own foundations before the builders could erect a beautiful two-bedroomed home with a terrace overlooking the valley.

Münstereifel proved to be a fairy tale-like town, with a medieval town wall, a moat and a crystal clear streamlet running through the centre, edged with local stone from which petunias cascaded on to the cobbled path. It is not surprising that after the *Wirtschaftswunder* (an economic miracle recovery) had helped to make some Germans more affluent again, the area became popular by weekend visitors from the industrial Ruhrland. The hill on which my aunts were the first to build a house soon sprouted more elaborate dwellings as weekend retreats. When Hanne and Grete found it increasingly difficult to manage their garden and climb up the hill, they were able to sell their property easily and profitably, assuring themselves of a comfortable living in Munich where other family members lived.

Our first trip to Germany also took us to Sennestadt, a new town built near Bielefeld after the war. It was the first time that Sylvia and Roman met their uncle, aunt and cousin Bettina. We had a lovely time there, as indeed we had done at our previous destinations. The children's German improved considerably.

Heartened by the relative ease with which our first trip to the continent ended, we took to the road again a couple of years later. This time the Beetle soared along the Autobahn to Heidelberg en route to Stuttgart and Munich, where I intended to introduce my family to more aunts and cousins whom I had not seen for many years.

It was in Heidelberg where we nearly lost Artur. We had managed to secure overnight lodgings in a quaint backstreet of the old town and were exploring our environment when the children spotted the first tram they had seen for a long time. 'We must take a ride. Please, please,' they begged. Artur decided to continue his tour of the historic town while we took a ride to the terminal of the Strassenbahn and back, arriving at our lodgings well after the children's usual bedtime. They were still bubbling over with excitement about their tram ride and all the things they had seen on the way, not forgetting the frankfurters and rolls with mustard on a little tray that we had eaten at the station while waiting for the return tram. But where was Artur?

Even Fräulein Huber, our landlady, was beginning to get uneasy when he had not returned by 11 p.m. There were no mobile phones in those days, but as a German speaker surely he could ask for directions if he had lost his way? However, this was complicated by the fact that he did not know where we were staying other than that it was a kind of terraced house in a backstreet with flower boxes at the windows – a description that applied to dozens of other places in a town like Heidelberg. The tourist office where we had arranged our accommodation was closed by then, too.

He did find our place eventually, having walked in circles at times and having gone up and down tiny streets till he spotted our car in the small parking space where we had left it. Fräulein Huber had switched all the lights in the front of the house on by then, which acted like a beacon and at last drew our lost sheep there.

While it was good to see my relatives in Stuttgart again and to introduce my family, it was sad to note how drastically uncle Fritz had changed. The once very smart and proud colonel was a shadow of his former self. He had never been well since he returned home after some years of forced labour in a Russian uranium mine. He died of lung cancer soon after our visit. Sylvia and Roman fortunately remember Stuttgart for more cheerful reasons. Being more or less housebound, Fritz had patiently taught his budgie to speak and perform little 'turns' at request. The children never tired of watching him.

More reunions took place in Munich, where Tante Lene and my cousin Hans and his wife had arranged a programme of outings to fill almost every moment of our stay. Munich itself was fascinating, with its Glockenspiel on the *Rathausturm*, the *Viktualienmarkt* where every conceivable item of fresh food, as well as preserves, spices, plants and flowers, wines and cordials could be bought. Spit roasted sausages were particularly appetising.

The underground train took us to the Starnberger See, which had bathing and boating facilities and huge ice cream cornets with vanilla flavoured whipped cream on top.

We also had Haxen and sauerkraut in the famous Hofbräuhaus and marvelled at the strength of the dirndle-clad waitresses who could carry at least half a dozen huge stone jugs with beer at any one time.

Hans had taken time off to be able to drive us to the Alpine regions of Bavaria to admire the lakes and mountains and the smart summer and winter sports resorts. Artur's camping stove made many a cup of tea to accompany picnics on wooded hillsides with glorious views over mountain ranges and well-known peaks like the Matterhorn and the Zugspitze.

Our next port of call was Bamberg, where another cousin lived with her family. Bamberg is a beautiful old town, full of medieval nooks and crannies, and historic buildings, including a castle and the Bamberger Dom with its famous statue, the Bamberger Reiter, which had been mentioned in our history lessons.

A day's drive along the River Main took us to the Rhein, where we spent the night in Assmannshausen, one of the many attractive wine villages in the region. Our room had a balcony overlooking the river. We could watch the large barges and passenger boats drift past while eating our potato salad and schnitzel, accompanied by local wine. The children loved their Malzbier, a sweetish dark beer with just a trace of alcohol. Boat watching and counting VW Beetles occupied the children as we drove down the scenic route towards the Autobahn and on to the hovercraft bound for Ramsgate.

We could not find a hotel room there and since it was a clear evening with not too much traffic on the roads we decided to drive home. I don't know how many miles I drove that day – I just about managed to stay awake till we reached home at three in the morning. Coco and Stipey, our cats, waited for us on the front door step – a sweet little reception committee.

We had acquired a red Beetle by the time that we set off for our most ambitious motoring holiday in 1976. I felt quite confident in driving on the continent by then. Luckily we had never encountered any major mechanical or other problems. Once the windscreen wipers ceased to function in an Alpine thunderstorm near Salzburg. We just had to sit it out and let the deluge pass, while thunder and lightning made us somewhat uneasy. In Aachen I scraped some paint off a Mercedes while trying to manoeuvre into the correct lane in a one-way system. The other driver accepted twenty marks for having the scratch painted out and then offered to guide us to the border via the least dangerous route.

Our twentieth wedding anniversary seemed to be as good a time as any to revisit Arbanats, a wine village near Bordeaux, where Artur's French friends lived and where we had spent part of our honeymoon.

We took a car ferry to Brittany first and were very impressed with St Malo. The Quiberon peninsula was very good for bathing. When dusk fell, we visited the Standing Stones in Carnac. There was an eerie atmosphere about the place, which made us wonder what provoked pre-historic man to put them there in the first place.

Mont St Michel was impressive and Pornic good fun for one evening, but the Cognac region was of interest only to Artur. Sylvia was sick and we sat in the shade of a large old tree while the men were rowed across the river to the Hennessy Brandy factory's visitors' centre.

We were made most welcome when we actually reached our destination. Madame Taste must have been in her fifties when my husband met her first while guarding an ammunition dump in the woods nearby. The German camp bordered on to the Taste's vineyards. It was inevitable that the family noticed the soldiers who had little to do other than reinforcing or erecting fences or, in Artur's case, writing unnecessarily elaborate notice boards warning the locals to stay away.

Madame Taste must have felt sorry for the polite young man who had actually spoken French to her when he asked for some water. She gave him water as well as wine and began to supplement his meagre rations with ladles of home-made consommé and fruit from the garden. They did not talk very much, but just accepted each other as human beings rather than enemies. In fact, the whole family, consisting of Madame and Monsieur Taste, daughter Odette and son Robert, were sad when the troops were withdrawn and the Americans began to reclaim occupied France. They asked Artur to get in touch with them once the war was over. So started a friendship through letters, which lasted over fifty years.

Madame Taste was eighty in 1976 – still a striking woman, slim and upright, with her hair swept back into a chignon, dressed in severe black. Youthful black eyes looked out of a careworn face. Her hands had obviously seen hard labour. I could not understand a lot of her fast-spoken French, but there was no doubt that she was delighted to see Artur again as well as 'Madame Rosemarie', as she preferred to call me, and our offspring.

She had been a widow for some years by then and Odette and Robert lived on the other side of Bordeaux with their families.

So she was alone on the old estate where she had spent all her life. The vineyards had been leased out some time ago and the house was obviously too big to maintain easily, even with some local help, but one could understand her reluctance to leave. There was something magical about the place and the wild garden in which herbs and diverse vegetables grew and peaches, plums and all shapes of tomatoes ripened in profusion. The large stone-flagged kitchen smelled of wood smoke, and tantalising scents emanated from the old cooking range. Odette had offered to bring some food along or to do the cooking, but Madame Taste insisted on doing it all herself as a matter of pride. She had obviously invested a lot of time, effort and imagination in this venture.

Aperitifs were served under the straw roof of the patio outside the kitchen, overlooking the colourful garden and the shed with the redundant wine press, old carts and barrels, now beginning to decay. The aromatic drink had been made at home from spirits and herbs, matured for a year or so, resulting in a very smooth liquid.

We made our way into the cool interior of the house after that. The best room, unused for many years, had been opened up for the occasion. The tiled floor was scrubbed, the Bombay commodes polished and the curvaceous antique French clock wound up and put in motion. It did not keep time any more, but the ticking of the brass pendulum and the quarterly chimes added to the quaint yet festive atmosphere of the environment. Bees hummed around the trailing roses that peeped through the open window.

The large table had been set with fine linen and napkins in silver serviette rings, the cutlery resting on crystal supports that matched the various drinking glasses. A silver basket was filled with colourful fruit from the garden and the dark grapes from which Monsieur Taste once produced his own brand of wine, 'Cru Capitayne'. Several bottles of this graced the table, in addition to the straw-coloured Barsac wine supplied by Robert's son.

There were ten of us at this dinner, with Artur seated in the place of honour between Madame Taste and Robert, who over the years had become the major correspondent with Artur and had visited us in England with his family.

Blanche, the hired help for the day, served the first course. It was the kind of consommé Artur had been offered in war days; a flavoursome broth with fine vermicelli and herbs. I could understand then that Artur's fond memory of this was not only of a sentimental nature. My own soups are usually good but this was superb. Then two large platters of fresh oysters appeared on the table, which a neighbour had collected at Arcachon that morning. Oysters had been one of the Monsieur Taste's favourite foods and were obviously much liked by the others, judging by the gusto with which they were consumed. Prize specimens were heaped on my plate too, and it would have been rude to reject them, in spite of my dislike of them. So I tried to enjoy them like everyone else did, but only just about managed to flush them down with copious draughts of the chilled Barsac wine.

By the time the pâté fois gras arrived I already felt distinctly light-headed, but enjoyed the house wine to accompany the delicacy.

A salad followed; luscious slices of tomatoes topped with sliced onions, herbs and the best French dressing I have ever tasted. The table became more animated by the minute as good food and Cru Capitayne did their work. Glasses were never allowed to become empty, so I was not sure how much wine I had drunk in the course of this leisurely feast. I did enjoy the guinea fowl, which arrived at the table to much acclaim, accompanied by delicate round French beans, fresh from the garden that morning.

However, I don't remember whether the glazed apple tart was good or not. I seem to have drifted off into oblivion on my high-backed chair, having at some point before that ceased to listen to the conversation around me.

I found myself eventually sitting on the old rocking chair on the patio in the fresh air, watched over by the amused other guests who had joined me outside.

'*C'est la vie*,' Madame Taste said later. 'I was glad you enjoyed our wine. Monsieur Taste would have been pleased to hear it.'

If it had not been for the oysters and all that Barsac, I might have stayed the course and saved myself acute embarrassment. I definitely did not set a good example to the children.

After the memorable time at Arbanats we wound our way via Biarritz, San Sebastian and Bilbao to Santander, where our ferry waited to take us back to England.

Air Travel

We acquired a taste for flying when taking advantage of one of the 'short break' offers of the early 1970s when Majorca was up and coming as a tourist resort for the British. The Germans had already established whole communities there and were having beer festivals, carnivals and masked balls in the resort next door.

Palms airport was still pretty much a field with some prefab buildings on, and in the Hotel Kontiki, the mortar had barely dried. From our balcony we could watch and hear the pile drivers and cement mixers building the next hotel on the row.

Still, who could complain? We thought that the eighty pounds we paid for the four of us for an all-inclusive break away from English February weather was quite a bargain. The Kontiki even had a swimming pool, much enjoyed by our offspring. It was pleasant enough to walk on the beaches and explore some of the island's interior, where the almond trees were in full bloom. Apart from visiting places where liqueurs and melon champagne were made, we visited a pearl factory and had sangria and a suckling pig barbecue in a cave. We felt that we had been away for weeks. It was actually snowing when we landed at Manchester airport.

When we tried to book a similar trip the year after, prices had more than doubled, because of the demand for short breaks and the fact that it was near to Easter. When Mavis in the Deansgate travel agency saw my disappointment she asked, 'Have you ever thought of going to Romania?' It had never crossed my mind, but my interest was aroused when she showed me the colourful little brochure she had just received from headquarters, advertising a totally new coach trip through Romania, which had not been on the tourist trail before. Because it was still of an experimental nature, the eight-day tour was very cheap – forty pounds per person – but it was certainly not nasty. I booked it there and then.

My family were rather sceptical when I mentioned that Bucharest rather than Majorca would be our Easter holiday destination, but warmed to the idea when I told them that Dracula's castle and cable cars in the Carpathian Mountains were on the itinerary.

We thoroughly enjoyed the unusual week once we had survived the very close scrutiny of the armed guards at the airport. First we stayed in an ornate Victorian style hotel in the centre of Bucharest, not far from the cathedral, where the whole population seemed to have gathered for the Easter Saturday candlelit midnight service. Incense and Gregorian chants filled the air as thousands of people lit their candles in the cathedral square.

It was a wonder that no one caught fire in the throng. Health and safety officials would certainly not have approved of such dangerous practices.

Our young, attractive tour guide, Eve, a university graduate, seemed daunted by the coach load of foreigners for whom she had been given a lot of responsibility. The route was pre-planned and the hotels had been booked, but she carried a purse for refreshments and meals en route, and for paying for visits of interest and evening entertainment on some nights.

It had been quite warm in Bucharest for early April, but as we drove northward it began to snow. Eve thought we should have some coffee before wading through the snow to Dracula's castle, from which we virtually slithered down eventually, so icy and steep was the hill. We stopped at a hotel in a small town where the staff was totally unprepared for an influx of a coach load of thirsty strangers. Someone was sent out into the sludgy street to buy some coffee since we did not fancy wine or slivovitz, the fierce local plum brandy, at eleven in the morning.

While we were trying to make ourselves comfortable in the rather dim, cold room, the manager summoned the resident gypsy band from their beds and in next to no time we were entertained by bleary-eyed violinists in their slippers with racy gypsy sounds and birdsong imitations, while we sipped some rather good coffee. They did deserve a tip and accepted it, although we had been told that tipping was not allowed in this 'socialist' state.

When lunchtime came we caught the staff of another hostelry unprepared and had to wait for what seemed an age for the potatoes to boil and the fish to be prepared. Eve realised at that point that it might be a good idea to forewarn innkeepers of our approach, to give them a chance to make some preparations. There seemed to be a dearth of vegetables, other than the potatoes and cucumbers that grew in huge greenhouses in the southern part of the country.

The hotels we stayed in were quite modern, apparently built for foreign visitors. Still, hot water was scarce and power cuts frequent in one or two of the places. However, we still seemed to be much better off then the local population who tended to live in very poor tenements in the towns. The painted churches in the northern province near the Russian border were fascinating but their rich interior contrasted almost perversely with the poor state of the villages around them. The nuns rushed around to fetch some intricately painted Easter eggs for sale and glowed with pleasure each time another one was bought with foreign money, which was much more valuable to them than their own currency.

In Poiana Brasow, an up-and-coming ski resort, we were able to take the cable car to the top of a mountain where there were the largest icicles we had ever seen. It is amazing that they did not dislodge the roof of the ticket office amongst the huge pine trees.

That evening we were driven to Brasow, called Kronstadt in Austro/Hungarian days, where time seemed to have stood still. Only a few gas lamps lit the huge snow-covered square with its solid, turreted town hall in the middle. Squat houses flanked the expanse, with shops already in darkness and only a few windows dimly lit. Horse hooves clattered on the cobblestones where the snow layer had been worn off by passing wheels. Our coach looked oddly out of place in this medieval environment.

A horse-drawn wooden carriage disgorged a group of young country folk who crossed the square excitedly, heading for a low door from which a shaft of light emerged. The men wore long boots and thick sheepskin coats, while the women had draped coloured shawls round their heads and shoulders, and exposed multicoloured petticoats as they lifted their skirts to skip over the slushy cobbles.

Shivering in the cold evening air, we moved in the same di-rection, drawn by the faint sound of music drifting up from the cellar. The scent of glowing charcoal and roasting meat intensified as we made our way down the wide, worn stone steps, soon to be enveloped in the warmth of a huge vaulted restaurant. A portly waiter with rolled-up sleeves and a leather apron beamed and bowed as he directed us to a rough scrubbed table, surrounded by wooden benches. Stumpy candles flickered and reflected in the tumblers and wine bottles, which were already waiting for us, along with fierce-looking, bone-handled cutlery. We were by no means alone in the cellar. There seemed to be people everywhere; drinking, eating and chatting in foreign tongues and furtively glancing in our direction once we had settled and were waiting for the things to come. We were surprised to have egg and bacon served as a first course – especially 'for the English', according to the waiter, but there was no doubt that most of us enjoyed the local cuisine even more. The spiced red cabbage complemented the succulent roast goose pieces perfectly and small sponge cakes, soaked with brandy made an unusual end to the generous meal. Wine flowed freely, each empty bottle being speedily replaced by a full one.

Soon even the most reserved members of our group thawed and entered into the spirit of the event, sighing nostalgically to the lilting gypsy tunes, and humming songs with vaguely familiar melodies from Viennese operettas. Feet began to tap when the colourful group whom we had seen at our arrival began to perform intricate folk dancing routines, which included toasts and invitations for all guests to sample the fiery local plum brandy. We did not understand a word of what was being said but this did not spoil the fun.

Harold from Stroud joined the dancers first and then a gypsy enticed Mary and Joan, two middle-aged teachers from Gloucester, to take the floor. Others joined in. It did not matter that no one really knew how to do the proper steps of the quite exotic dances which started slow but speeded up as the music increased in passion, accompanied by stamping, clapping and shouting.

The rather stolid group of other guests in sombre dark suits stared in amazement at the unbridled English, who contributed wholeheartedly to the general entertainment, when spotlights were switched on and cameras began to whiz to record all this merrymaking. Eve told us later that we were the first ever English tourists they had seen at the inn and that our stay coincided with that of a Russian trade delegation and a Japanese camera crew making a documentary about life in Romania in 1974. I just hope that they conveyed a more balanced picture to their Tokyo viewers!

We saw the vast beech forests of the Bukovina on the way back to Bucharest and drove through a very narrow gorge where the top of the bus barely escaped being damaged by icicles growing from an overhanging rock like stalactites. Tarom airways took us home safely at the end of this unforgettable week.

The More Serious Side of Life

While travelling during holiday periods was certainly interesting and educational, even relaxing at times, the rest of the year passed quite prosaically with the usual home and garden routines and professional work and study.

Sylvia and Roman did well at their local primary school and when the time came, passed their eleven-plus exams and the entrance tests for Direct Grant schools. Sylvia had to be kitted out with the red and gold striped blazer of Loreto College, while Roman gained a place in the then quite prestigious De la Salle College. They both went on to university later.

Artur's Manchester firm was taken over by a bigger concern, which meant daily travel to Liverpool for him and increased responsibilities, including a certain amount of travel for the firm, and later on behalf of the EU, as a member of a group of experts from the other member-states who were briefed to devise a manual of common terminology for the friction material industry. I came home from work at times to hear: 'No sandwiches tomorrow – I have a meeting in Paris, or Hamburg, or Turin, etc. His Stateless Travel Document made travel arrangements ever more difficult, so he applied for and gained British citizenship. For three pounds, a detailed application form and an oath sworn in Paul's office (our solicitor) I became British too, although I had never felt that my German passport was detrimental to my career development or elsewhere. As long as the expectations of my superiors were met I got the recognition I deserved.

Having worked for a number of years as a health visitor and school nurse in Old Trafford (some Manchester United football families were part of my caseload), I was asked if I would like to become a fieldwork teacher, an instructor and mentor for HV students. This meant going on a course in London to be familiarised with a new HV Training and Education syllabus and the new philosophy of the Training Council.

My family coped well with the help of Mrs Roberts, whom we briefed to look after the children after school and nursery hours. She did not consider it necessary to do any work in the house, because it was 'clean enough'. I took it as a compliment to me, since cleaning had never been a priority once my housemaid days were over.

I enjoyed the teaching aspect of my job very much and decided to do 'proper' teacher training when the opportunity arose. I was given a year's leave of absence without pay by my employer, and embarked on an intensive, year-long course at the Bolton College of Education, where well-established, professional people were given an opportunity to gain the Teaching Certificate of Manchester University.

So I crossed the Manchester Ship Canal daily on my way to Bolton to learn a lot more about teaching than I knew before. I was the only one of twelve students in my specialist group who had home and family responsibilities, so I had little time to join in the extra-curricular student activities, but enjoyed the experience of going back to school all the same.

At the end of the course I could not immediately find a teaching post which was compatible with home commitments, but I was welcomed back to my previous job with open arms.

A year later I was approached by a senior official of the Manchester Royal Infirmary, asking me to consider coming to teach in the prestigious nurse training school there. A new syllabus issued by the General Nurse Training Council (GNC) dictated that nurse trainees need at least a modicum of community experience in order to get a full picture of health service provisions both in and out of hospital. The post appealed to me since it tapped into the varied experiences I had had so far and I accepted it even though it meant taking a drop in salary from that of a Senior HV.

It was not easy to settle down in a new working environment, which was in some ways archaic and tradition-ridden. The old-established staff viewed an 'outsider' like me, who had not even trained in a 'top' hospital, with suspicion.

Still, the principal tutor welcomed new ideas and my particular background experiences. The students seemed to like the breath of fresh air that I felt I brought to the staid establishment. We even joked in the classroom at times and, when visiting a school clinic as part of their Community Module, we went to a pub to have some coffee (nothing stronger!) while waiting for the bus.

Needless to say, I did not endear myself any more with the other staff when I was offered a Senior Tutor's post, which others had coveted. Not expecting to get very far with my application, at the interview I had dared to say that I thought it was about time that trained personnel were allowed to take responsibility for their own actions, even go shopping in their lunch hour if this did not interfere with other commitments. Several of the six members of the interviewing panel had looked aghast – two others stifled a laugh.

So against all expectations, I became a 'Salmon, grade eight'. This had nothing to do with the quality of said fish, it just complied with the recommendations for staff grading introduced by the Salmon Report.

I had not read the small print on the job description and was rather taken aback when I realised that, apart from running the Community Module of the main course, I was going to be responsible for a part-time Enrolled Nurse course and was expected to deputise for the Principal – now a 'Salmon, grade nine' in her absence. I consoled myself with the thought that this was not likely to happen in the near future, but became rather panic-stricken when she told me that she was going on a month-long management course almost immediately, leaving me in charge of the school. This meant not only ensuring the smooth running of the study programme, but also close liaison with Matron (another 'grade nine' now) and other senior hospital staff, arranging interviews of staff and potential nurse trainees, and dealing with queries and complaints. Luckily, my secretary was well versed in the way that paperwork and statistics had to be presented to the General Nursing Council in London.

I dreaded the first of the staff meetings, which were held each Wednesday morning with tutors, clinical teachers, the librarian and the office manager, but found that a little humour helped to break the ice. We frequently got requests from abroad from people who wished to become nurses in England and that morning I had received a gem of a letter from an over-enthusiastic applicant: 'Dear Madame, only you can quench my burning desire to train at your esteemed establishment...' When I quite earnestly asked, tongue in cheek, if anyone thought we were capable of quenching a young Mauritian's burning desires, the twelve or fourteen folk present looked startled but then could not help bursting into peals of laughter. The rest of the meeting was quite amicable and I survived the remaining weeks of being the 'boss' without having a nervous breakdown.

My 'Salmon' days lasted just three years and reacquainted me with modern hospital practices as well as enabling me to learn a lot about tensions and relationships in a workplace.

It was this recent hospital experience on top of my public health knowledge that led to my appointment as lecturer at Manchester Polytechnic. They wanted a Health Visitor Tutor who could also run a part-time Clinical Teachers course. I seemed to fit the bill.

Another setting, new colleagues, new courses. I was glad that my Open University studies ended earlier than anticipated. I had been given to understand that while my previous qualifications earned me two 'credit exemptions', I would be required to gain four further credits to gain a degree. So it came as a surprise when after three years intensive part-time study I received a letter, inviting me to my own degree ceremony at the Free Trade Hall. 'You must be mistaken,' I wrote back. 'This is one year premature.' But there had been no error. I heard then that the half-credit courses I had chosen to pursue and my teaching qualification entitled me to another credit exemption, which nobody had told me about, releasing me from the hassle of another year's study at a time when I needed a lot of energy to meet the Polytechnic's demands.

When I sat in the Free Trade Hall in May 1975 to get my degree, a little note was passed down to me from the OU official whom I had corresponded with, querying what I thought to be my premature success. It simply said, 'Congratulations. I told you so!' It was a pleasing personal touch within an otherwise impersonal institution.

The degree definitely enhanced my career prospects, as I became a Senior Lecturer soon after.

'Head hunting' was at work again when after six years at the Poly, another post was offered to me – to become a lecturer at Bolton College Of Education, where I had actually done my teacher training ten years before.

Bolton Days

1979–1987

Joining the staff of BCET (Bolton College of Education, Technical) meant crossing the waters, this time, the Manchester Ship Canal, most working days. My little red Beetle chugged happily up the brow of the high level bridge and got me safely to Chadwick Street except when fog, ice, high winds or accidents caused delays or even blockages. When prolonged road works, intended to add an extra lane and strengthen the whole structure, were under way, there was often no alternative but to use the canal swing bridge – built in Victorian days, and solid and dependable. The only problem was that traffic came to a halt when a ship wanted to pass up or down the canal and the whole bridge had to swing ninety degrees to allow the vessel to sail past. The manoeuvre took only about twenty minutes or so but in rush hours caused mile-long tailbacks and associated driver frustration. I always took some reading matter along, in order not to waste valuable time. Still, such 'free' moments were not conducive to concentration on weighty matters, like exploring the latest fashions in educational theories, such as Bloom's *Taxonomy* or Gagne's *Conditions of Learning*. Neither of these had been talked about when I did my teacher training, but were the 'in thing' in the early 1980s.

The Bolton job as teacher of budding teachers turned out to be the most taxing, but also the most interesting one of my working life.

Apart from course planning, teaching and assessing in the college, it entailed a great deal of travelling during teaching practice periods, when my students' performances had to be appraised in their own teaching environment or, if not in post already, in a college which had offered a practice placement. Students from my specialist group (health visitors and district nurses) might spend their placements as far afield as Newcastle, London or even Cardiff.

Luckily, childcare issues were no longer a problem for me. Sylvia and Roman were at university by then. Artur did not mind my occasional absences when I took the sleeper to London for a day's work at North East London Poly or the North London College. I could at times be seen on Bermondsey Market at seven thirty in the morning and having a 'fry up' in a market cafe before winding my way to the South Bank Polytechnic.

I can't say that I enjoyed racing up the A1 at 7 a.m. to ensure I would reach Newcastle by 9 a.m., with a visit to Durham and Middlesbrough on the way back home. Still, I loved driving over the Snake Pass on sunny days on the way to Sheffield. Part of my job involved attending regular meetings in London of the National Nurse Training bodies and acting as External Assessor for courses in Scotland and Ireland.

I felt sometimes as if my feet never touched the ground. There certainly were very few dull moments, even on routine days spent at Bolton.

The following monologue gives a flavour of just one November day at college.

One of Those Working Days

I need not have washed the car yesterday. It is going to look worse than ever by this evening, after all. Gritty slush churned up by the lorry in front of me gives the windscreen wipers hard work to do and even then, the glass remains smeared and almost opaque in places. It is no joke driving to Bolton on a day like this.

I had set off early to avoid commuter queues at the high level bridge, but there is no getting away from commercial vehicles even at seven in the morning. St Peter's Way is clearer – not far to go now to Chadwick Street, towards the college. Luckily the car park is still fairly empty and I can choose a spot from where I can easily depart later when driving to Blackburn College to assess a teaching session of one of the sandwich course students. My red Beetle looks like a poor cousin next to Roy's top-of-the-range Celica.

I pick my way to the Admin Block across the slippery car park, hoping that my handouts have been copied. Beryl, one of the clerks, is in already and shares the latest college gossip with me over a cup of tea. The mail has not come in yet and my pigeon-hole is empty apart from a note from the new Principal, inviting me for a personal interview. He is seeing all staff members and is apparently very keen to hear that we all are engaged in further studies, doing research, or undertaking Master's degrees or PhDs. It takes me all my time to cope with day-to-day work! Betty is still off sick with stress and depression, so I have to look after her students, the district nurses, as well as my health visitor tutor group.

My office is in D Block, which means slithering over ice-coated flags which Jim, the caretaker, has yet to reach with shovel, sand and salt-filled bucket. The room is warm and welcoming but still too dark to manage without lights. I switch my desk lamp on and plug the kettle in. I need a cup of coffee and offer one to Hedwig, who is already waiting for me, having booked an early tutorial session. She looks cold and miserable. I believe it is much warmer in Hong Kong this time of the year. She is homesick and wonders why she let herself be persuaded to do a teacher training course in England.

This time she complains about the low grade she has been given by her Education Tutor for her last essay. She should have seen him, but he is off sick. Having dealt with similar essays before, I have a look at it and discuss with her how she could have tackled the subject. In essence, she had not really answered the main question of the essay. She seems to be a little more cheerful when she leaves to go to the lecture theatre for today's main lecture, where Jeff will be elaborating on Motivation Theories. This will be followed up by small mixed tutorial groups with a lecturer as facilitator. The idea is to help the students to try to apply the theories in their own teaching situations. I have an interesting group of twelve, not only nurses but also a couple of engineers and builders, and some from the office arts and hairdressing section – all experts in their own fields who wish to teach their subjects to others. I have learned a lot from them, especially in sessions involving skills analysis. I don't expect I will ever want or be asked to strip or assemble complicated machinery including Exocet missiles (!), but it is an education for me.

Mavis from the office was kind enough to bring my mail over and to make sure that I got the message from Blackburn which came while I was involved with the education tutorial. I don't mind at all that Jean's assessment session had to be cancelled for some reason, as it will give me an afternoon to catch up with long-overdue clerical work. I have already arranged for my own students to have an extra session in the AVA (audio-visual aids) department.

I brought a sandwich today, which comes in handy. No need to traipse over to the dining room for lunch.

At last I am able to finish next term's timetable, fill in the overdue expenses form for travels during recent teaching practice weeks and fix a time for interviewing applicants for the next course.

Some mail items are reassuring. The Course Tutors at Huddersfield and Leeds have once again agreed to take students for teaching practice next term. Early afternoon is not a bad time to get hold of Gail at Southbank Poly, who has yet to respond to my letter. She is actually able to take on a student who lives near London. I shall be glad when I have found practice places for the district nurses – we are in competition for these with the lecturer who runs the Technical Teacher Training course at Wolverhampton.

Four in the afternoon – getting dark already. I reckon I have done enough work for the day: I ticked more items of my 'to do' list than I dared to hope, and I still might just miss the worst of rush hour on the M63.

Well, Urmston, here I come. There has not been any more snow and luckily the heralded fog has not materialised.

Artur is out at a committee meeting of the Allotment Society tonight. I might get some assignments marked later. They have to be done before next week, ready for the Moderators' meeting at Jordanstown Poly (Belfast), where I am an external assessor.

Lights off at midnight. Tomorrow is another busy day.

College-related travels, 1987

Retirement party at Oakhurst, August 1987

Entertaining the Bridge Clan, Oakhurst, 1990

Retirement

1987

BCET had been a comparatively small independent college, with just over fifty able and dedicated staff members, whom it was not too difficult to get to know. This made for a most congenial working environment. Some of this individuality was lost when the college became part of a bigger unit – the Bolton Institute of Higher Education (BIHE).

A further reorganisation loomed when I had spent eight years there. It meant once again changing offices, allegiances with colleagues, revision of timetables, exam procedures and teaching practice organisation.

I had coped with similar upheavals in the past and there was no reason to believe that I could not rise to the occasion that time, but I was sixty by then and when I was offered a top-up of the pension, earned over thirty years in the health and education services, it seemed a good opportunity to consider retiring.

I realised that I would probably miss the hustle and bustle of busy days, but there was also much to be gained by having more time at my disposal. The prospect of avoiding almost daily traffic problems on the M63, where once again road works were in progress, was enticing. Burning the midnight oil while marking over-long student assignments would be a thing of the past. I would have more time to devote to family, home and garden. I might even get around to laying the stair carpet to the attic, a job that had been planned ever since we moved to Oakhurst, when the original family home became too small. I would have time for hobbies and interests, which had so far been marginalised. There would be time for travel, unencumbered by the constraints of the education year. I might even have time to relax!

My last student groups and my colleagues obviously had the latter in mind when they presented me with an elaborate sunlounger, an exotic plant for our patio and a coffee maker, as well as generous book tokens as leaving presents.

There was an official farewell dinner at 'The Last Drop', one of the well-known Bolton hostelries, which affected me more than I cared to admit at the time. Still, once I had cleared my office, returned overdue library books and handed in my keys, I suddenly felt a great sense of relief to have taken this step.

I suppose I also had good reason to feel a modicum of pride in my achievements. I had wanted to be a teacher even as a child and had reached that goal – in fact, more than I had anticipated. It had not happened in a planned way, but through taking opportunities as they arose and, needless to say, with a lot of hard work.

Well – Herr Seller had said all those years ago that I would have to work hard to earn my living. I actually enjoyed most of it.

Celebrating my sixtieth birthday and being a 'lady of leisure' was a good reason for having a party at home – for friends and colleagues whom I had met and kept in touch with over the years and who had been part of my life since I came to England nearly forty years ago.

The day could not have been more perfect for the get-to-gether. The garden was flooded with sunlight and the flower beds glowed with midsummer lushness. Colourful deckchairs were dotted about on the lawn and comfortable benches were placed in the shade of the sprawling ancient lilac tree.

Inside, the old kitchen table, draped in linen finery, was laden with party food, including a basketful of Danish pastries which I knew would find my guests' approval, since all of them had tasted these pastries at one time or other and had drooled over the exotic-looking little marzipan filled shapes. Who would have thought that a recipe found in *Woman's Own* in the 1950s would establish my reputation as an inimitable fancy pastry cook? On countless occasions I have been asked for the recipe and dealt out 'handouts' with illustrations, but everyone seems to have difficulties with the vagaries of yeast dough, which held no fear for me, having been brought up in a bakery and knowing that timing and temperature control are important to avoid unman-ageable sticky pastry and to produce feather light little mouthfuls.

Arthur and Doris from the Bridge clan came to the party, the first people I stayed with and worked for when I came to England in 1949. They had brought Lilian along, my tutor and later colleague at Park Hospital, very frail then and long retired and living near Hollingworth Lake, close to the Bridges.

Carla had driven over from Lincoln, where she now seemed to spend her time bossing her housemate about. She shared an office with me at Salford Health Department. Carla was still large and Teutonic-looking. She gave up health visiting when she and her supervisor realised that her forthright manner did not go down well with Salford folk, who needed subtle persuasion rather than didactic commands to become more health conscious where personal care and childcare were concerned. Luckily, she recognised her own limitations and had a great sense of humour. She actually recalled with mirth her second visit to our home when four-year-old Roman greeted her with: 'Aren't you the big fat lady who dropped the strawberry cake and cream on the floor when you came here last?'

Lisa, another Salford worker, was totally different, dainty and elegant, refined in every way. Her Jewish parents had sent her as a child to England just before the war and eventually she established a career like I did, through initial nurse training. She introduced her husband to us, a Welsh rugby club manager whom she had married when well over fifty.

Doreen was also there. She had stepped into my 'grade eight' post when I left the Manchester Royal Nurse Training School to start work at the Polytechnic, where I met Jenny and Pauline, two others who have remained good friends over the years.

A surprise visitor was Ann, my colleague and flatmate from London days. She just happened to be on a rare visit to the 'old country' from Canada. I had not seen her and her Greek husband for years.

She had never been to Oakhurst and fell in love with the place just as we had done some years ago, in spite of its multiple defects. Although if it had been perfect, we would never have been able to afford it. Fred, our architect friend, had said at the time that it was structurally sound but would require 'missionary zeal' to make it habitable and that he might have nightmares if he woke up in it. Even Paul, our solicitor, had voiced his concern: 'It is not overpriced, but do you realise what you are taking on?' He must have felt sorry for us because, once we had signed the contract, he offered himself and his old Jeep to take some of the smelly rubbish to the local tip. He never said so, but he must have regretted his offer when after five trips to the tip, still more debris was left, to be discarded at a later date.

Anyway, Fred, Paul and many others watched with interest, as the 'nightmare of a house' gradually became a very pleasant and welcoming family home.

As our guests drifted in during late afternoon, cool fruit punch was offered while they admired the garden. The background music, which Artur had laid on, was soon drowned by the babble of voices as folk re-established acquaintances. They all had met at one time or other.

Peter helped Artur to get the barbecue going. Soon the appetising scents of browning home-made hamburgers, sausages and chicken kebabs filled the air and tempted some of the guests to the kitchen, returning with chunks of home-baked bread and the staple salads of our parties: German potato salad, Polish bean and cucumber salad, dressed tomato slices – home-grown, of course – and so on. We still had a few bottles of Madame Taste's Bordeaux wine, too. This was as good an event as any to enjoy them.

When dusk fell, we lit the Chinese lanterns suspended in the lilac tree. It felt almost like my childhood birthdays. Then we sat in the mellow night air till late, enjoying the ambience.

Artur emerged from the cellar with my birthday cake. It was one of those irresistible nut gateaux, which had been a feature of many festive family occasions ever since Tadek and Artur baked one for me during Artur's and my courtship days. There were no candles on it – they might have melted the buttercream. It was as good as ever and provoked not only toasts to the 'birthday girl', but to absent friends, the shared past and to a new beginning.

Printed in Great Britain
by Amazon